# THE GARDENER'S YEAR MADE EASY

Which? Books are commissioned and published by Which? Ltd,
2 Marylebone Road, London NW1 4DF
Email: books@which.co.uk

British Library Cataloguing in Publication Data
A catalogue record for this book is available from the British Library

ISBN 978 1 84490 120 3

1 3 5 7 9 10 8 6 4 2

The publishers would like to thank Ceri Thomas and the *Which? Gardening* team,
Susie Bulman, Gemma Wilkinson, Danny Coope and Oliver Coupe for their help in the
preparation of this book.

Consultant editor: Ceri Thomas
Project manager: Emma Callery
Designer: Blanche Williams, Harper-Williams
Proofreader: Sian Stark
Indexer: Chris Bernstein
Printed and bound by Charterhouse, Hatfield
Distributed by Littlehampton Book Services Ltd, Faraday Close, Durrington, Worthing,
West Sussex BN13 3RB

Essential Velvet is an elemental chlorine-free paper produced at Condat in Périgord,
France using timber from sustainably managed forests. The mill is ISO14001 and
EMAS certified.

For a full list of Which? Books, please call 01903 828557, access our website at
www.which.co.uk, or write to Littlehampton Book Services.
For other enquiries call 0800 252 100.

# THE
# GARDENER'S
# YEAR
# MADE EASY

# ✿ Contents

# INTRODUCTION

Knowing what to do in the garden and when, is one of the trickiest things for even the most experienced gardener. This essential book covers all the jobs you really need to do during the year and leaves out the ones you don't, giving you more time to sit back and simply enjoy the garden.

Divided into the months of the year, the book is easy to use to discover what to do now. The jobs cover all parts of the garden, including borders, veg patch, fruit garden, lawn, pond and greenhouse, so you can go straight to the area you're interested in. To help you prioritise, we've broken each area of the garden into the jobs that are must-do and ones that are good to do if you have the time.

If you fancy a quick fix of gardening, but don't have much time to spare, look out for the five-minute jobs throughout the book. Then, when you've got a bit more time on your hands, be sure to try one of the monthly projects for the garden at the end of each chapter. They cover everything from taking cuttings to planting a colourful patio container. They're all explained in simple steps, so they're easy to follow.

Different pests and diseases can prove a problem at different times of year, so our pest and disease watch will leave you forewarned as to what to look out for each month and how to tackle it.

We hope you really enjoy this book and get a lot of use from it, month in, month out. The perfect size to pop in your pocket, it's a must-have for any gardener.

**ABOUT THE CONSULTANT EDITOR CERI THOMAS**
Ceri Thomas is Editor of *Which? Gardening*. She studied horticulture at the University of Reading and RHS Wisley, and is a passionate gardener.

# YOUR GARDEN IN JANUARY

Now you're no longer decking the halls, there's plenty to be getting on with outside. You can start improving your soil for this year's plants and crops, and take the time to plan what seeds you'd like to sow. Winter aconites and Christmas roses will lift the winter dreariness – especially after they have been tidied up.

# TOP JOBS THIS MONTH

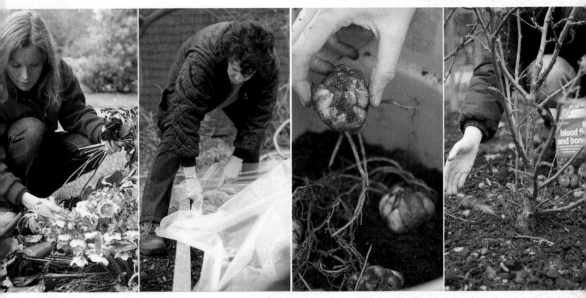

 **BORDERS**

Recycle your Christmas tree
Improve your soil
Plant winter aconites
Tidy hellebores
Cut out reverted stems
Turn off the water to outdoor taps
Buy seeds
Tidy up your shed

**IN THE GREENHOUSE**

Pick up fallen leaves
Check overwintering plants
Remove leaves from guttering

 **IN THE FRUIT GARDEN**

Mulch newly planted fruit trees
Plant new fruit trees and canes
Feed fruit plants

 **ON THE VEG PATCH**

Warm the soil in preparation for
planting outdoors
Harvest winter vegetables
Plant garlic
Buy onion sets
Watch out for moles
Plan carefully for what to plant where
in the months ahead

**LAWNS**

Keep an eye on your lawn as it may
need cutting
Remove grass cuttings as it's too cold
for decomposition
Service your lawnmower

 **PONDS**

Rake out dead leaves to prevent the
water stagnating

# ❀ Your garden in January

## BORDERS

### Must-do jobs
**Recycle your Christmas tree** Cut trees can be shredded and used as a mulch. If you haven't got access to a shredder, then contact your local council to find out about any recycling schemes they may offer. If you're taking the tree in your car to a recycling point, remember to put down protective plastic sheeting in the car or you will still be vacuuming needles when next Christmas comes around!

### Good to get done
**Improve your soil** If you have clay soil, dig in bulky organic matter – such as garden compost – and grit or coarse sand to improve the drainage. Only work on clay if the weather has been dry or it will be a sticky mess. For sandy soil, dig in plenty of organic matter to aid water retention. On chalky soil, add organic matter to increase the soil depth, aid water retention and improve the nutrient content. If you have very shallow soil, building raised beds gives more planting depth. Fill them with a mixture of compost, manure and good-quality topsoil. Organic matter added each year will gradually build up soil depth.

**Plant winter aconites** These are one of the first bulbs to flower. They look wonderful when established and they spread to form carpets of rich yellow flowers. It's best to buy new plants now while they're in growth as they are more likely to be successful than dry bulbs planted at other times of year.

**Tidy hellebores** Stop the fungal disease hellebore leaf blotch ruining the look of oriental hellebores (*Helleborus* x *hybridus*) by cutting off old leaves at ground level. New ones will soon appear to replace them. Try cutting off single blooms from favourite plants and floating them in bowls of water indoors where you can admire their delicate markings close up.

**Lift self-sown cyclamen**
*Cyclamen coum* form carpets of pink and white flowers that brighten up the ground under trees and shrubs during the winter months. Once established, they will often spread, aided by ants, which carry off their seeds. Look for the best seedlings with the most attractive leaf markings and replant them in a prominent place.

**Plant a pot with Christmas roses** Christmas roses aren't roses at all. They're a hellebore called *Helleborus niger*. Unfortunately, it's a rare event for them to flower for Christmas day but they make up for it with beautiful blooms early in the year. If you haven't had much success growing them in the ground, try planting them in a tall container instead, using John Innes No 3 compost. Gently tease the roots out before planting.

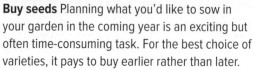

**Buy seeds** Planning what you'd like to sow in your garden in the coming year is an exciting but often time-consuming task. For the best choice of varieties, it pays to buy earlier rather than later.

**Have a tidy up** Sort out your shed, throwing away rubbish that has accumulated during the year. Clean and oil tools so that everything is in good working order when you need it in the spring. Sharpening blades on tools such as secateurs and hoes makes all the difference in how easy they are to use. Clean flower pots and seed trays – treat yourself to some warm water or it can be a cold and miserable job! It's also worth cleaning plant labels. A quick rub with a scouring cloth will remove old writing and saves you the cost of buying new labels. You can also make plant labels by cutting old plastic containers – such as yoghurt pots and plastic milk cartons – into strips.

## DISEASE WATCH!

**Leaf spot** Be on the lookout for this disease at this time of year as it can kill leaves. Simply cut off any infected leaves as soon as you notice them.

# 5 MINUTE JOBS

**Cut out reverted stems** – those that have fully green leaves – from variegated evergreens such as elaeagnus, euonymus or privet. These branches tend to be more vigorous than the variegated ones and if left to grow, can eventually take over altogether.

**Turn off the water supply** to outdoor taps and drain the pipes to prevent water freezing and pipes bursting. If this isn't possible, lag the tap instead. Also drain hosepipes and keep them free from frost by moving them to the shed or garage.

**Remove dead flowers** from patio pots, such as pansies and violas, to encourage more blooms.

# Your garden in January

## IN THE GREENHOUSE

### Must-do jobs
**Pick up fallen leaves or flowers** You should also remove dead plant material as leaving it around could lead to fungal disease and grey mould, which rots plants.

### Good to get done
**Check overwintering plants for damage** Take a look at any tender plants you're overwintering indoors and remove any diseased growth before it rots.

**Plant lilies in pots** Look ahead to summer by planting some lily bulbs in deep pots. Grow them on in the greenhouse and then use them to fill gaps in the border when they're ready to flower. You can also plant them directly in the border during February for flowers in the summer.

## 5 MINUTE JOB

**Remove leaves from guttering** Autumn leaves can block shed and greenhouse guttering, causing rainwater to overrun.

## IN THE FRUIT GARDEN

### Must-do jobs
**Mulch newly planted fruit trees and bushes** Well-rotted manure or rotted bark chippings are the best materials to use for this job. A thorough mulching around trees and shrubs will help to keep moisture in the ground and also prevents weeds from thriving too readily.

**Force rhubarb** The most expensive rhubarb to buy in the shops is the beautiful pink forced kind that appears early in the season, so it makes sense to grow your own if you can. In either January or February, cover your plants with a large lightproof container, such as a terracotta forcer or an old dustbin. A couple of shovels of manure will help to create extra warmth to speed up the process.

## Good to get done

**Plant new fruit trees, canes and bushes now** Make sure the soil isn't frozen or wet before planting. Add lots of well-rotted manure or garden compost to the planting holes. If the weather is poor when they arrive, pot them up or wrap the dampened rootball and store in a cold but frost-free shed.

**Feed fruit plants** During January or February, apply a general-purpose fertiliser, such as blood, fish and bone, to all tree, cane or bush fruit. Scatter the fertiliser on the ground in an area that is roughly equivalent to the spread of the branches. Gently rake it in to the ground.

## ON THE VEG PATCH

### Must-do jobs
**Harvest**
- ✿ Brussels sprouts
- ✿ Celeriac
- ✿ Jerusalem artichokes
- ✿ Kale
- ✿ Leeks
- ✿ Parsnips
- ✿ Sprouting broccoli
- ✿ Swede
- ✿ Turnips
- ✿ Winter cabbage

**Warm the soil** The weather can be unpredictable at this time of year. If the soil is cold and wet, do the digging and seedbed preparation later. To get the ground ready for early sowings, cover it with clear plastic sheeting, garden fleece or a cloche two or three weeks before you intend to make your first sowings. This will warm and dry the soil. It will also encourage a flush of weed seedlings that can be hoed off, meaning fewer plants to compete with your veg. Remove the sheeting or fleece just before you sow your early veg.

## Good to get done

**Plant garlic** Garlic is an easy and worthwhile crop, and one of the easiest to be self-sufficient in. If a bulb of garlic lasts you two weeks in the kitchen, plant two bulbs now. Don't be tempted to plant one that you've bought from a supermarket as the results can be disappointing. A garlic bulb should break into 10–12 cloves for planting. Plant these 15cm apart and each one will produce a bulb that will store until the following spring. Bury the tip to prevent birds pulling them out again. If the cloves push out of the ground as they grow, simply use a trowel to plant them deeper.

**Buy onion sets** Growing onions from sets is a far less fiddly way to raise onions than sowing seed. Look out for the small bulbs in garden centres now. Choose ones that are firm to the touch and store them in a dry place, ready for planting in March. 'Red Baron' is a good red variety, and 'Setton' and 'Jet Set' produce solid brown onions that store well.

**Watch out for moles** They tend to start to become more active because of mating and nest-building activity. The best way to control them is to trap them. Your local directory should have details of pest controllers in your area. Molehills make a useful source of topsoil.

**Plan carefully** Instead of buying and sowing the seeds of every vegetable you plan to grow, consider waiting to buy some young plants in late spring/early summer. Garden centres offer a good selection, or play safe and order by mail order now.

# ✿ Your garden in January

## LAWNS

### Must-do jobs

**Keep an eye on your lawn** Our increasingly unpredictable climate means we can get mild periods of weather even in the depths of winter. Grass is quick to respond to this mildness and puts on lush growth. As long as the ground isn't wet or frozen, it's a good idea to cut the grass, no matter how early in the year. It'll keep your lawn looking tidy and avoids the grass getting long and difficult to cut.

**Remove grass cuttings** If you mow your lawn, don't leave grass cuttings lying about – it's too cold and damp to allow decomposition. Collect cuttings and add them to the compost heap or put them in your green waste bin if your council provides one. A quick way to improve the appearance of your lawn is to redefine its edges using a half-moon edging tool or a spade. Compost the trimmings.

### Good to get done

**Service your lawnmower** Either do it yourself or book it in for a service with a local expert. Sharpen or replace the blades. Drain and replace oil, check spark plugs and clean air filters on petrol mowers. Check the cable and plugs on electric mowers.

# PONDS

## Must-do jobs

**Keep your pond healthy** Rake out any dead leaves that have fallen into ponds and water features that weren't netted in autumn. Leaves sink to the bottom and rot, clogging the pond and making it stagnant.

## HOW TO TAKE BASAL CUTTINGS

Cuttings taken from the shoots that arise from the base of clump-forming perennials are known as basal cuttings and are best taken from January through to early April. Among the tools listed to the left is a dibber. These are handy for making holes in the compost to insert cuttings into. You can buy them at a garden centre – or just use an old pencil.

### WHAT YOU WILL NEED

* Seed/potting compost
* A sharp knife
* A dibber
* Appropriate sized pots (9–10cm diameter)
* Labels
* Indelible pen
* Plastic bags or a propagator to maintain humidity
* Watering can

### How to do it

**1** Collect your cuttings. Select healthy, pest- and disease-free shoots. Cut off the chosen stems or gently pull them off from the base of the parent plant using a sharp knife.

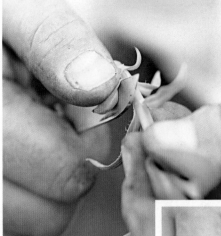

**2** Prepare your cuttings by removing the bottom leaves. Cut just under a pair of leaves as this will maximise the surface area available for rooting.

**3** Root your cuttings. Using a dibber, insert the cuttings in seed/potting compost, to half their depth around the edge of a 9–10cm pot. Label and water gently.

**4** After 4–6 weeks, roots should appear from the bottom of the pot. Pot the cuttings up individually into 9cm pots filled with seed/potting compost. After one to two months they'll be ready for bigger pots, or can be planted in the garden.

# YOUR GARDEN IN FEBRUARY

As winter starts to fade and spring gets ever closer, prepare for action by potting up rooted hardwood cuttings and repairing any broken fence panels and trellis. It's also the perfect time to start planting greenhouse crops, dividing snowdrops and putting up nesting boxes for the birds to use.

# TOP JOBS THIS MONTH

 **BORDERS**

Cut back ornamental grasses
Divide snowdrops
Feed the birds
Put up nest boxes
Hoe and pull up weeds
Take hardwood cuttings
Pot up the rooted hardwood cuttings from last year
Add some winter colour
Repair broken fences and trellis

**IN THE GREENHOUSE**

Start planting greenhouse crops
Start growing some of the earliest crops under cover
Sow slow-growing bedding
Start sweet peas
Plant peas in guttering

 **IN THE FRUIT GARDEN**

Plant new rhubarb crowns
Finish pruning fruit trees
Bring pot-grown strawberries into the greenhouse

 **ON THE VEG PATCH**

Start sowing seeds in warmed-up soil
Start chitting potato tubers
Plant Jerusalem artichokes
Invest in a soil thermometer

**LAWNS**

Repair any patches of uneven lawn

 **PONDS**

Melt a hole in any ice
Prevent further freezing by floating a ball on the water

# ❀ Your garden in February

## BORDERS

### Must-do jobs

**Cut back your ornamental grasses** By the end of January, ornamental grasses such as miscanthus can start to look a bit sorry for themselves. Now's the time to cut back the dead stems to ground level. Be careful not to damage the new green shoots that are emerging among them.

**Divide snowdrops** You can never have too many snowdrops – they are a welcome and cheery sight in the garden at this time of year. To increase your clumps, lift them as the flowers begin to fade and split them, replanting single bulbs a few centimetres apart. You'll have more success if you move snowdrops as growing plants than if you plant dry bulbs in the autumn. If you're buying plants, look out for spectacular large-flowered varieties such as 'Magnet' and 'Atkinsii'.

**Feed the birds** Many natural food sources run out at this time of year so it's important to provide extra food for birds. Tits enjoy hanging bird feeders but other birds, such as blackbirds and redwings, will feed from the ground – rotten apples are ideal. When choosing food, avoid wheat or barley, which only attract larger birds. Don't forget to provide a water source as well. To prevent diseases, wash feeders and bird baths regularly.

**Put up nest boxes** National Nest Box week runs in February. Organised by the British Trust for Ornithology (BTO), it aims to encourage as many of us as possible to add nest boxes to our gardens. Face your boxes between north and east to avoid the brightest sunshine and the coldest winds, and make sure there is an obstruction-free approach to the entrance.

## Good jobs to get done

**Hoe and pull up weeds** Spells of mild weather can see weeds appearing, so be vigilant and either pull them out or hoe them. The fewer weeds that manage to set seed now, the fewer weeds you'll have this summer.

**Pot up rooted hardwood cuttings** Hardwood cuttings such as dogwood (left) taken last year should have rooted and can be potted on or planted in the garden now. It's also a good time to take new hardwood cuttings. Many shrubs can be propagated this way, including fruit plants such as currants (see pages 34–5).

**Add some winter colour** There's no need for borders to look dull at this time of year. Look out for winter-flowering shrubs like this mahonia at the garden centre. They can be planted now for instant effect. Mahonia is a great choice as its spiky leaves are evergreen and in winter it has sweetly scented yellow flowers.

**Repair broken fences and trellis** It's good to do this while plants are dormant and there is therefore less foliage in the way. Repair any damage and erect new fences where necessary.

## IN THE GREENHOUSE

### Must-do jobs

**Start planting greenhouse crops** Veg such as tomatoes, peppers, chillies, aubergines and cucumbers need a minimum temperature of 18°C to germinate. A heated propagator is ideal, but if the background temperature in the greenhouse drops below 5°C, most will struggle, in which case you may prefer to wait until March. Alternatively, start them off on a well-lit windowsill until they are large enough and the greenhouse temperature is more predictable.

**Start some early crops under cover** It's still a long wait for the first crops of early potatoes, baby carrots, courgettes and salad leaves outdoors. However, you can look forward to early pickings by sowing (see pages 60–1) and growing them in large pots under cover in February. Keep the pots somewhere frost-free, with good light – a greenhouse is ideal, but a porch or well-lit shed will work almost as well. As the weather warms up, move the pots outdoors to start hardening off (see page 89). Keep the compost moist but not wet.

✤ **Courgettes** Sow a couple of seeds individually into a 7.5cm pot to start them off. When they have two proper leaves, transplant the best plant – one courgette plant should be enough at this stage – into a 15-litre pot.

✤ **Carrots** Fill a 15-litre pot with multipurpose compost, scatter the seed thinly and cover with a dusting of compost.

✤ **Broad beans** Sow them individually into 7.5cm pots for an early crop.

✹ **Salad** Scatter a salad mixture thinly and cover with a dusting of compost. There's now a good choice, including French, Tuscan and spicy mixtures, or you could buy the basic ingredients and mix your own.

✹ **Potatoes** Half-fill a 15-litre pot with compost and push a seed potato tuber into it. As the plant grows, top up with more compost until full.

✹ **Sow slow-growing bedding** such as antirrhinum, begonia, gazania, lobelia and pelargonium, and perennials and grasses to flower this year.

✹ **Start off sweet peas** For early flowers, sow sweet peas in a cold greenhouse in February.

## Good to get done

**Start peas** Peas are hardy and can be sown direct outdoors around this time of year. However, their seeds are tempting to mice and can rot in cold, wet soil, so it's better to start them off in a frost-free greenhouse. Sowing peas in a length of guttering has become a bit of a cliché, but but it does work really well.

✹ Look for flat-bottomed plastic guttering.

✹ Cut it into lengths that fit into your veg plot or raised beds, but that are no longer than about 1.5m.

✹ Block each end with bricks and three-quarter fill with compost.

✹ Sow the seeds in three rows about 5cm apart each way and cover with compost.

✹ Keep the compost just moist.

# IN THE FRUIT GARDEN

## Must-do jobs

**Plant new rhubarb crowns** in February in well-cultivated soil and mulch with strawy manure.

**Finish pruning** Cut back apples, pears, currants and gooseberries by the end of February (see page 201).

## Good to get done

**Bring pot-grown strawberries into the greenhouse or cold frame** – or cover any plants you have in the ground with a cloche – to encourage an earlier crop.

# ON THE VEG PATCH

## Must-do jobs
### Sow outdoors
✳ Broad beans, early carrots, peas, radishes, spinach, spring onions.

### Sow and plant indoors
✳ Aubergines, carrots, courgettes, cucumbers, peppers and chillies, potatoes, salad, tomatoes.

### Harvest
✳ Brussels sprouts, celeriac, Jerusalem artichokes, kale, leeks, parsnips, sprouting broccoli, swede, turnips, winter cabbage.

**Start chitting potato tubers** Stand the tubers in trays or egg boxes with the end with most sprouts uppermost and keep them in a cool, dry, frost-free place with plenty of light.

## Good to get done
**Plant Jerusalem artichokes** One of the easiest veg you can grow is the Jerusalem artichoke. Simply plant the tubers about 12cm deep and 30cm apart. They grow up to 2m tall and have bright yellow flowers so they make a useful windbreak for the back of the plot.

**Invest in a soil thermometer** This takes the guesswork out of early sowings. Check the temperature a couple of centimetres deep into the soil in the early morning. When the temperature is consistently above 5°C, it's safe to sow hardy crops – such as carrots, lettuces and radishes – into the ground.

## 5 MINUTE JOBS

**Cover your seeds** with cloches or fleece if you don't live in a mild area.

**Sow some lettuce,** including loose-leafed and red types, in small pots or modular trays (see page 60–1). Use them as fillers on the veg plot or even in ornamental borders.

# LAWNS

## Must-do jobs

**Repair uneven lawn** If you have a hollow or a raised bump in the lawn, it's an easy job to fix it.

❋ Using a half moon or spade, cut a capital H-shape in the affected area (1).
❋ Lift the turf and peel back the two flaps that you've cut (2).
❋ Either add additional soil to fill in a hollow (3) or remove excess earth in the case of a raised bump.
❋ Level the soil, then put the turf back in place and firm down (4).

# PONDS

## Must-do jobs

**Melt the ice** If your pond is frozen and contains fish, melt a hole in the ice by holding a saucepan of hot water on top of the ice to allow the fish and other pond life to breathe. To prevent the water freezing in the first place, put in a floating ball as it will help stop ice forming.

## WHAT YOU WILL NEED

- Woody, one-year-old stems
- Hormone rooting powder
- Secateurs
- 1–3 litre container
- Seed compost
- Spade/fork

# HOW TO TAKE HARDWOOD CUTTINGS

### What are they?
Hardwood cuttings are cuttings that are taken using mature wood – from either deciduous or evergreen plants – at the end of the growing season. Taking such cuttings is incredibly easy to do and they can even be planted in the garden to root.

### When to do it
November to February is the ideal time to take hardwood cuttings. The leaves of deciduous plants will have fallen off and the plant won't yet have started to form next year's leaf buds. You should get rooted cuttings in a year's time.

### How to do it

**1** Cut just above a bud, or pair of buds, where the current season's and previous year's growth meet. Trim the cutting to 20cm (if taken from a large tree or shrub) and 5-8cm (if taken from a smaller specimen). Remove leaves and side-shoots, but leave the buds.

**2** Next, you need to make two cuts: an angled cut, at about 45 degrees, just above the top bud; and a horizontal cut just below the bottom bud. Use a sharp pair of secateurs.

**3** To encourage rooting, use a sharp knife to wound each cutting at the base by removing a thin layer of wood. Dip the base in a hormone rooting powder.

**4** Fill a pot with seed compost and insert the cuttings around the edge of the pot, so that just the top buds are visible. Leave 5cm between each one so that they have space to grow.

**5** Alternatively, cuttings can be inserted direct in the ground, in a sheltered part of the garden or a coldframe. As a rule, they should be inserted so that only the top buds are visible.

**6** By the following autumn, cuttings should be well rooted and can be transplanted individually to their permanent positions in the garden or potted up to grow on.

# YOUR GARDEN IN MARCH

The weather's beginning to warm up and everything's coming alive, which means there's plenty to do in the garden pruning and feeding roses, planting bulbs, sowing seeds, planting vegetables and making a head start on dealing with weeds.

# TOP JOBS THIS MONTH

## BORDERS
Plant summer-flowering bulbs
Prune and feed roses; plant a new one
Tie in climbing roses
Cut back coloured stems
Cut back perennials that had been left for winter interest
Prune buddleia
Plant sweet peas
Sow hardy annuals
Deal with weeds
Feed borders

## IN THE GREENHOUSE
Maximise sunlight
Sow seeds
Create new plants
Repot succulents
Pot up plug plants

## IN THE FRUIT GARDEN
Feed fruit
Cut back blueberries
Prune raspberries and gooseberries

## ON THE VEG PATCH
Sow veg outdoors
Protect early sowings
Plant onions, shallots and potatoes
Sow salads and herbs
Plant out peas

## LAWNS
Remove weeds and treat bare patches
Prepare grass for mowing

## PONDS
Keep water clear
Plan a pond if you don't have one

## BORDERS

### Must-do jobs
**Plant summer-flowering bulbs**

While their spring-flowering cousins are putting on a show, it's time to think about planting summer-flowering bulbs such as camassia, alliums, crocosmia or eucomis, gladioli and dahlias. Look out for them at the garden centre. Check bulbs feel firm to the touch and don't have any signs of mould. Many can be planted now where you want them to flower but some should be started off indoors – check the packets for details. Like all bulbs, they prefer good drainage, so put a handful of grit at the bottom of the planting hole.

**Prune roses** Cut any rose bushes and hedges back by one third to a half. Cut diseased stems back to healthy growth. Prune established bush roses removing crossing, dead and damaged wood, and prune the main stems to an outward-facing bud around 15–20cm from ground level. Finally, cut the sideshoots of climbing plants back to three or four buds.

### PEST WATCH!

**Slugs and snails**
All that lush new growth is a magnet for slimy marauders.

We've found that slug pellets based on metaldehyde and organic pellets based on ferric phosphate are equally effective. Or, try biological controls for slugs or barriers such as copper tape (now also with serrated edges) to protect container plants or use WD40 on non-porous pots.

**Tie in climbing roses** Check over climbing roses and tie in old or new growth that's not attached to the support. Remember to ease it down to as near horizontal to the support as possible as this encourages it to produce flowers over the whole length of the plant, rather than just the top where it's difficult to see them.

**Feed your roses** Get your roses off to the best start by feeding them with a specialist rose fertiliser. They're heavy feeders so it's a good idea to make a note to feed them again in midsummer when they're developing their second flush of flowers.

**Cut back coloured stems** Willow (salix) and dogwoods (cornus) grown for their coloured winter stems should be pruned now. Cut each stem to an outward-facing bud within 5cm of the old wood, although weaker growers such as *Cornus sanguinea* 'Midwinter Fire' should only have a third of the stems cut back. If you want larger willows and dogwoods, prune every other year. You can either keep your prunings to use next month as supports for herbaceous perennials or shred them to add to the compost heap. Remember always to wear gloves and safety goggles when shredding.

# ✿ Your garden in March

**Cut back perennials if left for winter interest** Traditionally, perennials were cut back in the autumn after their summer display faded. But more and more gardeners are leaving the job until spring so they can enjoy the dead stems covered in frost during the winter. Now's the time to cut any remaining stems back to make way for the green shoots that are beginning to push through the earth. Most plants should be cut back to ground level and the stems composted. However, if you grow penstemons, hold off on cutting these until May or new growth could be hit by frost. After pruning, apply a fertiliser and mulch bare soil with organic matter such as garden compost.

**Prune buddleia** Keep these potentially enormous shrubs in check by cutting back all of the stems to about 30cm above ground level. Prune stems to just above a pair of buds.

## 5 MINUTE JOB

**Deadhead daffodils** Removing the flowers as they fade will make the bulbs put their energy into next year's display instead of making seeds. Don't cut back the foliage yet – wait until it has turned brown when it can be easily pulled away.

## Good to get done

**Plant sweet peas** Sweet peas sown indoors last month should now be ready to be planted outdoors. If you haven't done so already, pinch out the main growing tip to encourage sideshoots to break out from the base of the plant. Then plant them in a sunny spot and provide something for them to grow up. They'll eventually cling on by themselves using their tendrils, but they need tying in with string to get them started. If you didn't

have time to sow sweet peas in pots indoors earlier in the year, don't worry, as if you live in a milder area, they can now be sown outside where you want them to flower.

**Sow hardy annuals** Get hardy annuals such as calendulas off to an early start by sowing them in module trays. Sow a few seeds per module and then thin them out to the strongest seedling. This is not only a great way to get a head start but is also easier than sowing direct where they flower, which can produce very patchy results. However, if you do want to plant annuals such as pot marigold and love-in-a-mist outside where you want them to flower later in the year, remove any weeds and stones from the sowing area and rake until the soil has a fine surface. Always sow the seeds in a recognisable shape so it's easy to differentiate between seedlings and weeds.

**Deal with weeds** Weeds will be starting to burst into growth just like everything else in the garden. A hoe makes short work of clearing a large area. Aim to skim just below the soil surface to sever the weed tops cleanly from the roots. Always hoe on a sunny, dry day to prevent the weeds re-growing after you hoe. When the ground is cleared, apply a layer of mulch to suppress further weed growth. Chipped bark is good for preventing weed seedlings appearing when applied 5cm deep. Perennial weeds, such as dandelions, which will regrow from their roots, are best killed with a weedkiller containing glyphosate.

**Feed borders** Give your borders a spring boost by applying a general-purpose fertiliser.

**Lift hellebore seedlings**
Hellebores cross-pollinate with other varieties and self-seed readily. Dig up seedlings and pot them up to grow on – you may discover a new variety.

**Take cuttings of delphiniums and lupins**
Use new shoots emerging from the base of the plant and cut them from just below soil level with a sharp knife. Insert the cuttings into pots containing John Innes No 2. Put the pot in a clear plastic bag and the cuttings should root in a few weeks.

### Deadhead camellias

Many camellias hang on to their flowers once they've turned brown with age or have been hit by frost. Unfortunately, the only way to make your plants attractive again is to remove these blooms by hand.

**Deadhead violas** For the best results, you should remove viola flowers as they fade for a continuous display of blooms from October to May. If you can't face this time-consuming job, we found that it was best to leave plants untouched rather than cutting them back.

## PEST WATCH!

**Viburnum beetle** *Viburnum tinus, V. lantana and V. opulus* are all favourites of the viburnum beetle. This annoying pest nibbles their leaves from spring to autumn. Keep an eye out for the creamy yellow caterpillars feeding on new leaves and remove any caterpillars that you find.

# ❀ Your garden in March

**Plant a rose** New potted roses should be in the garden centre now and it's a great time to plant them. Water them thoroughly and dig a hole that is deep enough so that when planted, the bud union (the nobbly bit on the base of the main stem) is about 2.5cm below ground level. Add some soil improver to the base of the hole and firm your plant in firmly using the toe of your boots.

**Show off bamboo** If you've got a bamboo with coloured stems, such as this golden one (left), why not show them off to their best advantage? Simply cut off the lower leaves on each stem to reveal the coloured canes beneath. A suitably coloured background will show them off even better.

## Plant perennials

Fresh new perennial plants should be arriving in the garden centre. They're perfect for filling any gaps that are revealed after tidying the border. As they're perennials, they'll return each year and, if you buy several smaller plants, they're a quick way of creating a real splash of colour.

**Remove pampas flowers** After years in the fashion doldrums, pampas grass seems to be making a comeback. If you haven't grown it for a while, try one of the varieties with delicate, drooping flowers such as *Cortaderia richardii*, and plant it in the border rather than 1970s' style in the middle of the lawn. If you have a pampas grass already, now is the time to remove the fluffy flowers, cutting them at the base to make way for new growth. The foliage is quite coarse, so wear gloves if you've got sensitive skin.

**Protect plants** Spring is well on the way and the weather is getting warmer, but your garden can still be hit by frost in March. If frost is forecast, use fleece to protect the new leaves of hydrangea, Japanese maple and pieris. You can protect any emerging seedlings the same way. You should also cover the flowers of apricots, cherries, currants, peaches and plums – if they get frosted, you won't get any fruit. For large plants, cover as many branches as you can. Uncover on frost-free days to allow pollination.

## IN THE GREENHOUSE

### Must-do jobs

**Maximise the sunlight in the greenhouse** Keep the glass as clean as possible to maximise the amount of light reaching young seedlings.

**Sow seeds** There's not much to beat the thrill of seeing the first seedling appear from a pot you've sown only a few days (or months!) before. Now's the time to get started sowing bedding and veg plants indoors. Check the packets for sowing times and don't be too eager to sow everything at once or you'll have millions of seedlings all needing your attention at the same time (see also pages 60–1).

### Still time to ...

✿ **... sow indoor tomatoes.** It's best to wait until now in unheated greenhouses. Germinate seeds in a heated propagator at 21°C.

**Look after veg in pots** Early vegetables that were sown last month in pots in the greenhouse should be coming along and will be well ahead of this month's first outdoor sowings. As the potatoes grow, keep adding more compost until the pots are full. This encourages more tubers to form and stops them being pushed out of the compost later and turning green. If conditions aren't yet suitable for sowing outside directly into the ground on the veg plot in your area, start some more containers to follow on.

## 5 MINUTE JOB

**Open greenhouse vents**
On warmer days, it's worth nipping out to the greenhouse and opening the vents. This will improve ventilation and will help to avoid problems with fungal diseases. Don't forget to shut the vents in the afternoon, though, as spring nights can continue to be surprisingly chilly.

## Good to get done
**Create new plants** If you potted up dahlia tubers in February, now is the time to take cuttings from them. Use a sharp knife to remove some of the shoots the tuber has produced and then cut them just under a leaf with a slanting cut. Carefully remove the bottom leaves and put them into a pot of gritty compost to root. You should then find that both the original tubers and the cuttings will flower this summer (see also pages 22–3).

## DISEASE WATCH!

To avoid disease, check over your plants regularly and remove any leaves or flowers that are going mouldy to stop the problem spreading.

**Repot succulents** If your succulents need more space to grow, repot them in free-draining compost now. Mix the compost 50:50 with grit. Either wear thick gloves or use an old padded envelope to hold the plant when repotting sharp cacti and agaves.

**Sow tender herbs** such as coriander and basil indoors (see pages 60–1). Wait for warmer weather before sowing them outside.

**Replenish container compost** If you have long-term residents such as bay trees in your containers, scrape away the top few centimetres of compost. Replace it with fresh compost.

**Pot up cannas** Cannas add a tropical touch to the garden. Their lush leaves and brightly coloured flowers make them well worth looking out for. You'll find them on sale in the garden centre now, ready for potting up. Keep an eye out for signs of the canna virus (streaked leaves) once it's growing.

**Pot up plug plants** The first plug plants (seedlings that have been grown in individual cells) will start arriving now. Take them out of their packaging as soon as they arrive, water and pot up within 48 hours to avoid stunting their development.

**Move on seedlings** As soon as seedlings become large enough to handle, move them into new trays of compost or pots at wider spacings. This will give them extra room and allow them to develop properly. When handling the seedlings, hold onto the leaves, never the stems, which are easy to crush. Use a pencil or dibber to loosen them from the compost (we often refer to this as pricking out).

**Get plants for free** Have a look for a few 'free' plants at the garden centre. You'll find many perennials offer the chance to create extra plants for free as you can divide them when you get home. This hosta should give four plants for the price of one. When dividing your plants, make sure that each new piece has leaves and roots. Pot up and water well.

## IN THE FRUIT GARDEN

### Must-do jobs

**Feed fruit** Blackcurrants, plums, cherries, cooking apples and pears all appreciate a dose of high-nitrogen fertiliser such as sulphate of ammonia now as they're hungry feeders.

**Cut back blueberries** Begin by taking out any spindly or dead stems. Once the bush is three years old or more, remove one or two of the oldest branches to ground level as these become less productive with age.

### Good to get done

**Harvest forced rhubarb** Remove light-excluding covers from forced rhubarb. When picking rhubarb, pull off the stems rather than cutting them, as cutting can let in infection.

**Prune raspberries** Cut old canes of autumn-fruiting raspberries down to ground level when new shoots start emerging from the soil. Shorten tips of summer-fruiting varieties if they have outgrown their supports. Mulch with organic material, such as garden compost, but don't bury newly planted canes too deeply.

**Prune gooseberries** Gooseberries are such easy-going fruit that we often neglect them. Pruning will help to keep your plants in shape and help to avoid problems with mildew by allowing air to circulate more easily. Cut back sideshoots to a bud about 8cm from their base and prune the tips of branches back to within three or four buds of the new growth. It's also worth thinning any shoots that are crowding the centre of the plant as this will make it easier to reach in and pick the fruit. The main stems can also have the new growth they made last year cut back by a third. After pruning, feed and mulch your plants and they'll be set for summer.

# ON THE VEG PATCH

## Must-do jobs

### Sow outdoors
🌼 Beetroot, chard, peas, early carrots, parsnip, turnip, kohl rabi, spinach, spring onion, radish
🌼 Lettuce, herbs, salad leaf, including oriental greens

### Plant outdoors
🌼 Early potatoes

### Sow indoors
🌼 Greenhouse aubergines, cucumbers, melons, peppers and tomatoes
🌼 Outdoor tomatoes – start in the greenhouse or indoors
🌼 Celery and celeriac – start in modular trays under cover and sow on the compost surface as they need light to germinate
🌼 Leeks and onions and shallots as an alternative to sets (see page 19); sow thinly in seed trays and thin out later
🌼 Brussels sprouts, summer cabbage, calabrese, cauliflower
🌼 Broad beans in pots

### Sow veg outdoors
After months waiting to get going, it's full steam ahead on the veg patch as many popular vegetables can be sown now (see pages 60–1). If the weather has been very wet or cold, hold back and wait for conditions to improve. Covering the soil with plastic in the meantime will help warm up the ground (see page 18).

### Still time to ...
🌼 ... **plant Jerusalem artichokes** (see page 32).

53

**Protect early sowings** Fleece or clear polythene should still be used to protect existing seedlings and to warm up the soil before sowing (see page 18). Some vegetables – beetroot, for example – can run to seed if sown too early without protection.

## Good to get done

**Plant onions and shallots** Onions aren't expensive to buy in the shops, but all the same, it's relatively easy to be self-sufficient in them for most of the year. Work out how many you need from late summer to the following spring and simply plant that number. Although you can grow onions from seed, they're easier from sets (small, half-grown bulbs), available in garden centres now. There are two types: untreated and heat-treated.

* You can plant untreated sets from early March, just as soon as the soil starts to warm up and isn't too wet.
* Or plant heat-treated sets in April. The heat treatment reduces the risk of the plants bolting.
* Both onions and shallots will be ready to harvest in late summer and they should store through to early spring. (Bolted onions don't store, but can still be used fresh.)
* Shallots have a sweeter taste and cost more to start with, but store for ages. Use a trowel to avoid damaging them as you bury them – about 15cm apart in rows 30cm apart, or 23cm apart each way in raised beds.

**Plant potatoes** Towards the end of March plant out early potatoes, such as 'Accent' and 'Red Duke of York' that started chitting in January. Wait until April in cold areas. You don't have to dig a trench when planting potatoes. Use a spade or trowel to bury individual tubers about 15cm deep. A potato planter will make the job even easier. Apply a mulch of well-rotted garden compost – this will be incorporated into the soil by worms and also as you earth up the rows. Alternatively, plant at the bottom of a large tub and gradually top up with compost (old compost is fine) as they grow, to prevent the tubers going green. Check the weight of the tub and water when it feels light.

**Sow salads** You can now sow the first short rows of baby leaf salads outside. If you opt for individual types, sow separate rows of each as they grow at different rates. Scatter slug pellets sparingly or use other slug and snail controls to protect the tiny leaves. Unless your garden soil is free of weed seeds, sow baby leaf salad in raised beds or containers containing multipurpose compost. To save money, part-fill with garden soil and top up with the compost. Salad leaf can be a nightmare to weed!

**Sow annual herbs** Start with hardy types such as parsley, chervil and chives. Parsley can be tricky to germinate – be sure to use fresh seed and cover the row with fleece to keep it cosy until seedlings appear.

**Plant out peas** Harden the peas sown in guttering in February (see page 31) for a week or two and then plant out in the veg patch. Using a draw hoe or something similar, make a shallow trough the same depth and width as the guttering. Carefully slide the compost out without disturbing the pea seedlings. Draw soil up either side of the compost to fill any gaps. At the same time, sow another band of peas direct into the ground to provide a second crop 3–4 weeks later. Horizontal strings around canes help peas climb upwards.

**Plant out broad beans** If you started them in pots in the greenhouse earlier in the year, plant them out now. You could also sow a second batch direct into the ground to prolong the harvest, but unless your soil is warm and well-drained, it's best to start these off in pots too. Space plants 20cm apart in double rows or in blocks. Support them using posts if necessary.

### DISEASE WATCH!

**Brassica downy mildew** Remove any brassica leaves that begin to turn yellow. This will help to prevent the spread of grey mould and brassica downy mildew.

**Sow brassicas** Sow calabrese, summer cauliflowers and Brussels sprouts now in a greenhouse or a sheltered spot outdoors. Use 7cm-pots or modular trays filled with multipurpose compost. The best modern varieties are all F1 hybrids so the seed is expensive but germination is usually very good. Re-seal the packets and keep the spare seed for next year. Bear in mind that hybrid cauliflowers produce their heads over a short period of time. Make several sowings of a couple of plants, or as many as you can eat in a fortnight, every two to three weeks to spread the harvest. Calabrese will produce lots of side-shoots and can be harvested over a longer period.

**Catch crops** At this time of year there's plenty of spare ground on the veg plot. Areas set aside for tender crops that will be planted later, such as larger members of the cabbage family, tomatoes, courgettes or dwarf beans, can be used for a quick or 'catch' crop. Sow short rows of radish, spring onion, spinach or chard, oriental greens such as mizuna and mustards or lettuce. They should be ready before the later crops are planted out in May, but if you leave space for the late crops, you can carry on harvesting the catch crops while they are settling in. Also plant out lettuces started in pots last month. Protect them with a thin scattering of slug pellets.

**Feed spring cabbage** Use a high-nitrogen fertiliser such as Growmore or pelleted chicken manure to give plants a boost. When you harvest the cabbages, cut them off and make a cross-shaped cut in the top of the remaining stem. This will encourage a second crop of mini cabbages to form.

**Planning for succession** Rather than sowing long rows of each veg and expecting them to crop over a long period, try sowing short rows every fortnight or so for a succession of harvests. That way, you should have a regular supply of veg at their tender best. This works well for beetroot and carrots, lettuce and other salads, and for peas and dwarf beans, which crop over a short period.

**Dig in green manure** If you have sown some green manure in August (see page 151), now is the time to chop it with a spade and dig it in.

# 5 MINUTE JOB

**Support pea plants** and keep the pods off the soil. The traditional method of using twiggy branches is ideal because when it comes to composting the remains of the crop later, you can just add the twigs to it. Match the height of the support to the variety.

## LAWNS

### Must-do jobs

**Remove weeds** It's not just the grass that gets growing again at this time of year, unfortunately the weeds are busy too. Spot treating them now before they've had a chance to flower should help to limit their spread. Either dig them up by hand (an old knife is useful for big weeds such as dandelions) or use a chemical spot treatment.

### Good to get done

**Prepare grass for mowing** If you didn't do it in September, use a spring-tine rake to remove moss and thatch (dead grass), preferably before you do your first mow. Leave the mower blades on their highest setting for the first cut.

**Treat bare patche**s Prepare areas for sowing or turfing. You can lay turf now but wait until April to reseed.

**Mow the lawn** The grass is probably looking rather unkempt by now, so if you get a spell of dry weather, nip out and cut the lawn on a high setting to tidy it up.

# PONDS

## Must-do jobs

**Keep water clear** Remove any remaining dead foliage and let it dry at the edge so that any trapped wildlife can make its escape.

## Good to get done

**Plan a pond** Now is a good time to construct a new pond because newts and toads will be seeking new breeding grounds. Alternatively, you may want to fill in an existing pond leaving the liner in place and turn it into a bog garden instead. That way, you'll still be able to grow water-loving plants, but you won't have the worry that your pond will dry out in times of drought and hosepipe bans.

**Check your electrics** Check and clean filters, pumps, water features and lighting systems.

## 5 MINUTE JOB

**Feed fish** As the pond warms up, the fish will appear to search for food. If the water temperature is between 5 and 8°C, feed with a winter food. You should really remove any uneaten food after five minutes to avoid poor water conditions and sick fish. Once the water temperature starts to get over 8°C, fish can be fed with a high-protein summer food.

# HOW TO SOW SEEDS

Making new plants is cheap if you grow them from seed. Seeds often cost just a few pence or you can collect free seeds from plants (see page 148). Fellow gardeners will also often have leftovers in their seed packets.

## Outdoor sowing

**1** Make a seed bed by forking the soil and removing weeds. Rake to give a crumbly surface and a level site. Firm and rake again.

**2** Using a string line, draw a shallow drill using a pencil or dibber. The depth of your drill will depend on the seed so check what depth and spacing you should sow to beforehand.

**3** Sow seeds thinly by taking a pinch of seed from your hand and sprinkling it into the prepared drill. Draw soil back over your sowings, then lightly firm the soil and water.

**4** When seedlings appear, thin them to allow those remaining to grow stronger – again, check the seed requirements for the amount of space your plants will require to grow well.

## Indoor sowing

**1** Start off with a small container such a seed tray, pot or modular tray and fill with compost. If the compost is lumpy, crumble it between your fingers to avoid any air pockets. Tap the container so that the compost settles evenly and level off any excess.

**2** Firm the compost down into your container – this will enable water to rise around the seed and will reduce the number of air pockets, which should help with germination. Sow your seed thinly over the surface of the compost at a spacing of about 5mm.

**3** Cover the seeds with vermiculite (to the equivalent of thickness of the seed). This will keep the compost moist and will help the seeds that need light for germination. Label, water carefully and pop into a plastic bag. Place on a sheltered windowsill or in a heated propagator.

**4** Once your seedlings have developed a pair of leaves and it's feasible to move them, prick them out (lift out) using a cane, pencil or dibber.

**5** Using a dibber or pencil again, make a hole in the cell of a modular tray. Hold the seedlings by their seed leaves so as not to bruise the stem. Insert the root system in the hole. Gently firm in, water and place in the propagator or on a windowsill to grow on.

## Tips

**Sowing small seeds** Mix dust-like seeds with dry silver sand to aid sowing as it'll show where you've sown.

**Sowing large seeds** Sow two per pot and thin out the weaker one when it comes to potting on. Or put single seeds in single cells of modular trays.

# YOUR GARDEN IN APRIL

Now that spring is well and truly here, there's plenty to keep you busy. Lots of different veg seeds can be sown directly into the ground, some spring flowers will need deadheading, your border plants could do with a feed, and it's time to mulch fruit trees and bushes and tidy strawberry beds.

# TOP JOBS THIS MONTH

## BORDERS

Feed borders
Prune spring-flowering shrubs
Prune for foliage
Take leaf cuttings
Plant out hardy annuals
Give support to tall perennials
Mulch around shrubs
Divide plants
Plant evergreens
Cut off dead hydrangea flowers
Deadhead bulbs

## IN THE GREENHOUSE

Sow herbs
Plant up greenhouse crops
Take cuttings
Care for plug plants

## IN THE FRUIT GARDEN

Mulch fruit trees and bushes
Give citrus plants a boost
Plant raspberry canes

## ON THE VEG PATCH

Sow maincrop root veg for winter
Sow catch and tender crops
Thin seedlings
Deal with weeds

## LAWNS

Rake the lawn
Apply fertiliser and grass seed

## PONDS

Remove blanket weed
Divide overgrown pond plants

## BORDERS

### Must-do jobs

**Feed borders** Now spring is here, plants will be putting on plenty of new growth and so will benefit from feeding. Give your plants a boost. Use a general-purpose fertiliser such as fish, blood and bone, hoe into the surface and then cover the earth with a 5cm-layer of mulch – bark and grass clippings both work well. If the weather hasn't warmed up, delay mulching or you'll trap the cold in the soil. Don't be tempted to be generous by applying more than the packaging recommends as you could burn the delicate new shoots.

## Still time to ...

❄ ... **plant summer-flowering bulbs** (see page 40).
❄ ... **protect shoots**, especially those young hosta leaves, from slugs and snails (see page 40).
❄ ... **prune roses**. Remove dead growth, feed with a rose fertiliser, and mulch (see pages 40–1).

**Prune spring-flowering shrubs** Wait until their display begins to fade and then get them in shape to encourage an even better display next year. Deciduous shrubs, such as forsythia and flowering currants, should have the stems that have just flowered cut back to strong, young shoots lower down. It's also worth removing about 20 per cent of the older stems at their base to encourage new growth. Lavenders benefit from a light trim to stop them getting leggy and woody.

**Prune for foliage** A trick to get extra large leaves on foliage shrubs such as smoke bush (cotinus) and elder (sambucus) is to cut them back hard each spring. This technique is known as stooling and involves cutting the shoots back to within a few buds from ground level. This will encourage them to produce vigorous, young growth with beautiful leaves. If you don't want to lose all the height the plant gained last year, leave two or three shoots unpruned. It's best to feed and mulch the plants after pruning to give them a boost.

# ✿ Your garden in April

✿ **... sow hardy annual seeds**. The soil's now warm enough in most areas to sow seeds directly into the ground. Sow hardy annuals such as pot marigolds, love-in-a-mist, candytufts, cornflowers, sunflowers and nasturtiums where you want them to flower (see also pages 60–1)

## Good to do

**Take cuttings** You can take cuttings of new shoots of tender plants, such as busy lizzie, coleus, diascia, fuchsia, pelargonium, trailing petunia and verbena, at this time of year. Remove shoots from the base of your chosen plant with a sharp knife, cutting just below the bottom pair of leaves. Trim the end of the cutting and dip it into rooting hormone. Put the cuttings into moist, gritty compost and place them in a heated propagator if you have one, or on a sunny windowsill. Spray with water regularly to prevent wilting until they root.

**Plant out sweet peas** Plant out sweet peas sown in autumn and tie them in to supports – see below.

**Give support to perennials and plants that tend to flop**
Put in supports before the new growth of perennials gets too large as there's less likelihood of damaging the delicate shoots. In addition, lupins, delphiniums, campanulas, chrysanthemums and other flowering border plants become top heavy when in flower and can easily be flattened by windy weather. Pea sticks are very versatile plant supports. If you have difficulty getting hold of them, try border restraints such as bamboo canes with twine, Y-stakes, or netting instead. Don't worry if the supports look a bit obtrusive at first – your plants will soon grow through.

**Mulch around shrubs** Help trap the spring moisture in the ground by mulching around shrubs. It's particularly important to pay attention to camellias, rhododendrons and azaleas as their flowers next year can be affected by how much water they receive the year before. Before you apply the mulch, apply some general-purpose fertiliser.

**Aphids** Squash them or treat with a spray containing bifenthrin or pyrethrins.

**Lily beetle** Watch out for the bright red adults and black, gunk-covered larvae – they will strip lilies and fritillaries of their leaves and blooms. Remove any you find or spray your plants with a suitable insecticide.

**Divide plants** Dig up the plants and divide them into smaller pieces, each with its own roots and leaves (see pages 206–7).

**Pick up a bargain at the garden centre** Garden centres will be fully stocked at this time of year. If you can bear the crowds, it can be a great chance to pick up special offers designed to tempt customers in. Go early in the day before things start to sell out and take a list of what you want to buy to avoid temptation.

**Top five weeds to look out for** Weeds will be growing faster now as the weather warms up. Dandelion (1), bindweed (2), hairy bittercress (3), cleavers (4) and creeping yellow cress (5) are worth dealing with now, before they take hold. Weed borders little and often, and hoe weed seedlings on dry, sunny days so they shrivel and die and don't re-root. For problem weeds such as couch grass, you'll have to dig down with a trowel or hand fork and follow their spreading roots, teasing out as much as you can.

**Plant evergreens, perennials, container-grown climbers and late-summer bulbs** Now is the time to plant evergreens such as phormiums, cordylines and bay, and new evergreen hedges. Planting perennials now means they will have time to establish while the weather is still mild and wet. You can also plant unsprouted dahlia tubers and gladioli now – but wait until next month for dahlias in colder areas.

**Keep a lookout for self-sown plants** Aquilegia, alchemilla, foxgloves, primroses and bronze fennel tend to pop up everywhere. Move them to where you'd like them to grow, or, if you have too many, pot them up and give them to friends and neighbours. Also look for self-sown tree seedlings, especially native trees such as hawthorn, blackthorn and spindle – these can be transplanted and made into a native hedge that will help create a habitat for wildlife.

**Continue to rejuvenate clumps of perennials and grasses**
Established plants can become congested, which will make them flower poorly. Lift them, divide the clump discarding any old growth and dead material, then replant the healthy sections in soil that has been dug over and some fertiliser added to the hole. Either chop the clump with a spade or cut it with a garden knife or old kitchen knife.

**Cut off dead hydrangea flowers** Shorten thin or old shoots of mophead and lacecaps (*H. macrophylla*) to their lowest bud. To get larger flowers on *H. paniculata*, cut main branches to within two buds of their base.

**Cut back lavatera hard** Lavatera benefits from being cut back hard in April. Cut all of last year's shoots back to the base of the plant; new shoots will soon appear, which will carry this summer's flowers.

**Check roses for suckers** Tear off (don't cut) shoots growing from below the point where the variety is grafted onto the rootstock (a lumpy bit on the main stem) to prevent weakening of the plant.

# 5 MINUTE JOBS

**Deadhead spring bulbs** Boost next year's displays of spring bulbs such as daffodils and tulips by removing the flowers as they fade to conserve the plants' energy. Do this as soon as the flowers fade but let daffodil leaves die off naturally. Don't cut them down or tie them up when flowering is over – when they turn brown, they should pull away easily.

**Tie in climbers** Encourage blooms from top to toe by tying in new growth on climbing plants as near to horizontal as possible.

## IN THE GREENHOUSE

### Must-do jobs

**Sow herbs** If there are some herbs you just can't get enough of in the kitchen, then save money and sow lots from seed instead of buying individual plants. Herbs that can be sown now in the greenhouse or on the windowsill include basil, parsley, chives, marjoram and dill (see pages 60–1).

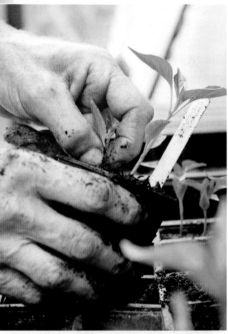

**Plant up greenhouse crops** As greenhouse tomatoes, aubergines, peppers and cucumbers start to fill their original pots, move them into bigger pots. If you sowed several seeds per pot to start with, remove surplus ones or carefully separate out the individual plants and give them their own 7cm-pot. Hold them by the seed leaf rather than the stem to avoid damaging them and try to keep as much root as possible. Fill the new pot with compost, make a hole with a dibber, or your finger, and drop the roots in. Firm the compost around the plant and water it in. If you started the seeds off in a propagator, carefully acclimatise them to the greenhouse temperature by leaving the lid off and then move them.

## Good to get done

**Take cuttings from lupins and delphiniums** The new shoots of lupins and delphiniums can be used to make new plants by taking basal cuttings (see pages 22–3).

**Care for plug plants** Plug plants are still likely to be arriving. Remove them from their packaging as soon as they arrive and pot up within 48 hours.

**Sow flowers** Check seed packets for sowing dates and remember to keep checking seedlings so they're pricked out before they grow leggy (see page 51).

**Water seedlings** Keep a check on seedlings as they're particularly vulnerable to drying out, especially when the weather gets warm. Keep some fleece at hand to cover them if cold nights are forecast though.

## 5 MINUTE JOB

**Damp down the greenhouse floor** Bright sunny days can set the temperature soaring so damp down the floor with water and open vents and windows.

## IN THE FRUIT GARDEN

### Must-do jobs

**Mulch fruit trees and bushes**
Ensure new or established trees and bushes are well mulched to help keep weeds down, and keep moisture in. Ensure that the mulch doesn't lie against stems, canes or trunks as this may encourage diseases and cause the stems to rot. Well-rotted manure is ideal – check out local or city farms for a supply.

### Good to get done

**Give citrus plants a boost**
Begin feeding citrus plants once a week in April with a citrus food.

**Feed blackcurrants**
Although you might have fed blackcurrant, hybrid berries and blackberries in March, they will still appreciate a high-nitrogen feed, such as sulphate of ammonia, now.

**Tidy strawberry beds** Lay a bed of straw around the plants, ready to keep the developing fruit away from slugs. During the day, open cloches to allow insects in to pollinate the flowers.

**10 MINUTE JOB**

**If frost is forecast,** protect the flowers of fruit trees and bushes as well as those of strawberries by covering them with fleece (see also page 18).

**Last chance to plant raspberry canes** Once they are planted, cut the canes to 15cm above ground level. Erect a support system using posts and wire, drape with netting to prevent birds and then mulch.

# ON THE VEG PATCH

## Must-do jobs

### Sow outdoors
❀ Maincrop carrots, beetroot, parsnip, swede and turnip for winter
❀ Catch crops – beetroot, chard, early carrots, turnip, kohl rabi, peas, spinach, spring onion, radish, lettuce, salad leaf, including oriental greens and rocket

### Sow indoors
❀ French and runner beans
❀ Courgettes and summer squash
❀ Pumpkins and winter squash
❀ Sweetcorn
❀ Outdoor tomatoes, if not done last month
❀ Leeks, if not done last month
❀ Brussels sprouts (if not done last month), sprouting broccoli, kale
❀ Calabrese and cauliflower
❀ Tender herbs such as coriander and basil

### Harvest
❀ Baby salad leaves
❀ Spinach
❀ Oriental greens

**Thin seedlings** Give seedlings space to grow. Remove any excess so that plants are at the spacings recommended on the seed packets.

**Deal with weeds** Just like in your flower borders, as the soil starts to warm up, weeds will start to germinate. This is a clue that hardy veg will also germinate, but unless you control the weeds, your crops will have to cope with the competition. To keep them at bay, see page 44.

### Good to get done

**Plant onions** If the soil was too cold or wet in March, plant your onion sets now. Heat-treated sets are best planted this month too (see page 54). Onions and shallots started from seed last month will resemble grass at this stage. You can plant them out now or leave them to thicken up. Don't waste spare onion sets or shallots. Plant them close together in pots and snip the young shoots with scissors for an early crop of salad onions. Plant whole garlic cloves in pots on the kitchen windowsill and snip for a fresh garlic flavour to add to dishes.

**Sow dwarf beans** In mild areas, you can sow dwarf beans and sweetcorn seeds outdoors under cloches or fleece. In colder parts of the country, it would be best to wait until May before sowing outside.

**Keep sowing catch crops** The short rows of catch (fast-growing) crops you sowed last month will be appearing now. There should still be plenty of space to sow some more and if you want a constant supply of tender baby carrots, chard, baby beets, radish, spring onion, spinach, oriental greens or lettuce, keep sowing little and often. As the weather warms up, catch crops will grow faster. Try sowing a new batch of crops once the previous one has emerged rather than adhering strictly to the calendar.

**Cut-and-come-again** The baby salad leaves should be ready for the first cut and the first home-grown meal of the year. Use scissors to cut about 2cm from the soil or compost level and carefully remove all the cut leaves. The cut stumps should produce a flush of new growth in a couple of weeks. Keep them moist and if they start to look pale, feed with a dilute high-nitrogen fertiliser. Make a second sowing now, which will continue cropping after the first sowing starts to decline, and so on through the summer.

## Plant out brassicas

Calabrese is fast growing and should be ready to plant out now. With flowering brassicas such as calabrese and cauliflowers, take care not to disturb the roots when transplanting – any check to growth can cause them to produce under-sized heads. Space calabrese 30cm apart each way if you want main heads and a succession of side-shoots. You can make further sowings for a succession of main heads.

## PEST WATCH!

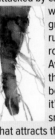

**Carrot fly** Carrots and parsnips can be attacked by carrot fly whose grubs ruin the roots. Avoid thinning because it's the smell that attracts the flies. Damage can be reduced by intercropping them with onions or cover with a fine mesh.

**Mice** love newly sown peas and broad beans and work along the rows – use traps or bait if they become a nuisance.

**Pea and bean weevils** nibble the leaf edges of young pea and broad bean plants, but rarely cause serious damage. Covering new plantings with fleece will help keep them out until the plants are large enough to fend for themselves.

**Plant maincrop potatoes** These are traditionally planted around Easter, but as this varies from year to year, mid-April is a safe bet. Space rows 75cm apart and individual tubers 38cm apart for the maximum yield. Aim to use up early maincrops such as 'King Edward' before Christmas. Late varieties such as 'Cara' should store until well into the spring. If blight (see page 136) is a persistent problem, go for 'Sarpo Mira' or 'Sarpo Axona'.

(see page 136)

## Still time to ...

🌿 ... **plant shallots, onions and garlic**. Leave their tips just protruding from the soil and keep an eye out for birds pulling them up.

**Earth up early potatoes** Do this when the first shoots reach about 15cm. Gently draw soil from either side of the row over the centre, covering all but the tips. Use a draw hoe or a soil rake – if the soil is too hard to rake, break it up first with a fork. Keep doing this at intervals until you end up with a low mound roughly 30cm high and across. This helps increase the number of tubers and prevents them being pushed out of the soil and turning green and poisonous later. The shoots are very vulnerable to late ground frosts. If air temperatures of 2°C or below are forecast, cover the rows with fleece.

## Sow root veg for winter

If you want root crops for winter – carrots, beetroot, turnip, parsnip and swede – sow now direct into the ground in rows 30cm apart. Sow carrot, turnip and swede seed thinly and for parsnips, place a couple of seeds at 15cm intervals – even with fresh seed, germination can be slow and erratic, so don't hoe until the seedlings have emerged.

**Sow tender crops** You can wait to sow all these tender crops direct outside when the soil is warmer, or get a head start and sow in pots in the greenhouse (see pages 60–1). You still can't transplant them until there's no danger of frost, so wait until early May in the coldest areas; otherwise mid- to late April should be fine.

- **Climbing French and runner beans** Sow the large seeds individually in pots. Don't sow too many climbing beans – a wigwam of just 12 plants can yield 12kg!
- **Courgettes and squash** Sow the large seeds individually into 7cm-pots. Two courgette plants should be plenty for most families; expect up to 30 fruits from each. Winter squash will give 3–8 fruits, depending on the variety, weighing up to 10kg a plant, but beware: the plants can be rampant spreaders.
- **Dwarf French beans** can be sown individually in small pots or modular trays. Or save time and sow 4–6 seeds together in a 7cm-pot and plant out as clumps.
- **Sweetcorn** Each plant will give one or, if you are lucky, two decent cobs but over a fairly short period in late summer. To ensure good pollination, plant groups of at least 12 plants at a time. Sow seed individually in pots.

**Sow tender herbs**
Sow tender herbs such as basil and coriander now. If the soil is still too cold outdoors, sow the first batch in containers under cover (see pages 60–1). Bear in mind, though, that basil doesn't transplant well. You don't have to wait until

hardy herbs sown last month produce large plants. You can treat them as cut-and-come-again once individual leaves are big enough.

**Move veg outdoors** It should be safe to move hardy veg such as salad leaf and carrots outside now. Tender crops such as courgettes and potatoes in pots can be stood outside during warmer weather, but watch out for frosts. Water regularly to keep the compost just moist.

## 5 MINUTE JOB

**Cover calabrese and cauliflowers** straight away with fleece or fine mesh to keep the main pests out, particularly flea beetle, which damages the young plants, and caterpillars that can burrow right into the flower heads.

## LAWNS

### Must-do jobs

**Create a lush lawn** Thicken up your turf by 'overseeding' thin patches. Rake the lawn to remove dead grass and moss then apply a general-purpose fertiliser and thinly scatter grass seed. Buy a small pack of grass seed rather than one of the lawn repair kits on the market. April is also a good time to start a new lawn, either by sowing seed or laying turf (see pages 172–3). If you are seeding, cover your lawn with netting to protect it from birds.

### Good to get done

**Rake out moss** – you can use it to line hanging baskets if it hasn't been treated with weedkiller.

## PONDS

### Must-do jobs

**Remove blanket weed** to let oxygen in. Green gloop invades ponds in warmer weather. Fish it out by hand, with a plastic rake or try a blanket weed treatment. To reduce the problem, add plants to your pond so that some water is shaded by leaves.

### Still time to ...

✳ **... scoop out leaves** to prevent them from decomposing and affecting the nutrient balance of the water.

### Good to get done

**Divide overgrown pond plants** Irises, water lilies, reeds and rushes will benefit from being divided at this time of year. Replant them in baskets of aquatic compost topped up with gravel. Take care not to damage the pond liner when cutting iris roots.

## HOW TO TAKE LEAF CUTTINGS

Taking a leaf and putting it in compost is such a satisfying way of making a new plant and it also has the distinct advantage of costing next to nothing.

### What are they?

Cuttings taken from plants that have thick, fleshy leaves or lack stems so are unsuitable for other methods of propagation. There are two types of leaf cuttings: leaf sections and whole leaves.

### When to take them

At any time of year as long as the leaves are free of pests, diseases and blemishes. Check they are the current season's growth.

### WHAT YOU WILL NEED

- A clean, sharp knife
- Cutting board
- Seed compost
- Seed trays or pots
- Labels
- Indelible pen
- Propagator or plastic bags to maintain humidity
- Dibber (or pencil)
- Growbag

### How to take whole-leaf cuttings

**1** With a sharp knife, remove a healthy leaf and at least 1.5cm of the stalk. Avoid leaves that are too small, have blemishes or any sign of pests or disease.

**2** Insert the leaf stalk into a pot or tray of compost at a 45-degree angle – it's important that the leaf does not shade the new plants that will develop at the base of the leaf. Place in a plastic bag or propagator.

**3** In approximately eight weeks, you should be able to see baby plants growing at the base of the leaf (the new growth is actually coming from the base of the leaf stalk). Carefully separate each new plant from the parent, being careful not to damage the delicate roots. Pot up each new plant individually.

### Plants this technique is suitable for

- African violets (Saintpaulia)
- Hoya
- Peperomia
- Sedum
- Jade plant (Crassula ovata)

## How to take leaf-section cuttings

**1** Remove a healthy leaf from the parent plant using a knife. The size of the leaf isn't too important as you'll be cutting it up later but avoid leaves that are very small, have blemishes or have any sign of pests or disease.

**2** Lay the leaf upper-side down on the cutting board and cut it into pieces the size of a large stamp. Alternatively, the whole leaf can be used. Each portion should have a vein down its length. Gently nick the vein without cutting through the leaf.

**3** Place the leaf sections on a pot or tray of compost. Cut a 2.5cm length of wire and bend it so that when it is pushed through the leaf, the nicked veins come into contact with the compost surface. Water from above and label.

**4** Place cuttings in a plastic bag or propagator. They will take 8–12 weeks to root and shoot; new plants will emerge eventually from the cut veins. Once they're big enough to handle, pot them up individually into 9cm-pots.

### WHAT YOU WILL NEED

* A clean, sharp knife
* Cutting board
* Seed trays or pots
* Seed compost
* Labels and indelible pen
* Small amount of garden wire
* Propagator or plastic bags to maintain humidity
* Dibber (or pencil)

### Plants this technique is suitable for

* *Begonia rex* – whole leaf and leaf sections
* Cape primrose (streptocarpus)
* Christmas cactus (schlumbergera) – best inserted vertically into the compost without the need for cutting leaf veins
* Gloxinia – whole leaf
* Mother-in-law's tongue (sansevieria) – whole leaf

# YOUR GARDEN IN MAY

May is one of the highlights of the gardening year. Frosts will soon be a distant memory, the days are longer and the soil is warm. This month's essential jobs include hardening off plants, tying in sweet peas and clematis, shading glass in the greenhouse to prevent it from overheating and – if you grow it – harvesting asparagus spears.

# TOP JOBS THIS MONTH

### BORDERS
Catch weeds early
Harden off plants
Plant dahlias
Keep an eye out for pests
Tidy up tulips
Feed spring bulbs
Sow hardy annuals outdoors
Cut back ivy and ceanothus
Deadhead flowers
Protect plants from slugs and snails
Tie in clematis
Check soil pH

### IN THE GREENHOUSE
Shade glass and check temperature
Get watering
Take cuttings
Repot tomatoes

### IN THE FRUIT GARDEN
Net soft fruit
Mulch strawberry plants

### ON THE VEG PATCH
Sow beans, peas and quick crops outdoors
Protect tender veg on cold nights
Plant greenhouse crops
Erect supports for beans and peas
Plant courgettes and squash
Sow winter crops
Transplant leeks

### LAWNS
Mow the lawn
Use lawn clippings to mulch borders

### PONDS
Plant water lilies

## PEST WATCH!

**Aphids** Squash them or treat with a spray containing bifenthrin or pyrethrins (see page 70).

**Cats and squirrels** Protect new plantings from animal digging – surround with a frame of pea sticks, chicken wire or upturned hanging baskets.

**Lily beetle** Continue to watch out for these bright red adults and black larvae (see page 70).

**Viburnum beetle** For more information, see page 45.

**Vine weevil** If patio plants suddenly wilt and start to die, vine weevil grubs could be to blame. If the plant isn't too badly damaged, pick out all the creamy white grubs from the soil and repot in fresh compost. Treating the soil with a nematode biological control will put a stop to further damage.

## BORDERS

### Must-do jobs

**Deal with weeds** Weeds will be growing as fast as your plants now so try to keep on top of them by hoeing your garden once a week. Choose a dry day so they wilt and die and keep your hoe sharp. Remember that perennial weeds such as dandelions need to be dug up or sprayed with glyphosate to kill their roots or they'll quickly resprout.

## Harden off plants

Plants raised indoors must be acclimatised to colder temperatures before they're planted outside. For a week, take the plants out of the greenhouse during the day and bring them inside at night. Then leave them outside at night too, but cover with horticultural fleece or put them in a cold frame with the lid closed. Do this for about a week. Your plants will then be 'hardened off' and can be planted out in the garden. If there's a chance of frost after your new plants have been planted out, cover them with fleece. Also keep some fleece handy to protect Japanese maples, hydrangeas, fruit blossom and tender vegetables including potatoes.

**Plant dahlias** Dahlias can be planted out towards the end of the month. Cuttings taken earlier in the year should be ready, alongside potted and bare-root tubers. As dahlias make heavy plants that need supporting, put in a sturdy stake next to each planting hole. Slugs love the young shoots, so use controls now – non-organic and organic pellets both work well, as does biological control.

## Good to get done

**Tidy up tulips** after flowering, once the foliage has died down. As they begin to fade, be sure to snap off the dead heads before they have a chance to make seed. This will encourage them to concentrate their energy on producing next year's blooms. If your soil is free draining, the bulbs can be left in the ground. If it's heavy, lift bulbs and store them in a cool, dry place for replanting in November.

**Mark bulb positions with a stake.** As early flowering bulbs die back, insert short canes or sticks around their clumps to mark their position – this will help you avoid accidentally damaging dormant bulbs.

**Feed spring bulbs** Look forward to colourful displays next year by feeding your spring bulbs with sulphate of potash or tomato feed while they're still in leaf, as they're busy making next year's flowers now. Don't cut down the leaves until they naturally turn yellow as they're needed to make food for the bulb – similarly, never tie the leaves in knots to tidy them up.

**Continue to plant bulbs** Plant summer-flowering bulbs, corms and tubers such as dahlias and gladioli.

**Top-dress plants in containers** Remove the top layer of compost and replace it with new compost mixed with a slow-release fertiliser.

**Sow hardy annuals outdoors** If you sowed hardy annuals such as calendula in module trays in the greenhouse earlier this spring, now is the time to plant them outside. Don't worry if you didn't get a chance as there's still time to sow the seeds directly where you want them to flower. Before sowing, make sure you remove all weeds to reduce competition and make it easier to find your seedlings when they emerge.

**Prune topiary** Topiary shapes such as balls and cubes are fun and attractive in the garden. The first flush of spring growth may have left them looking a bit shaggy by now so give them a quick trim. Regular snipping is a much easier way to keep them looking neat rather than giving them an annual overhaul.

**Cut back ivy and ceanothus** Clip over the new growth on box and conifers with a pair of topiary shears, cutting back to just above the old growth. Cut back ivy on fences and walls, and from windows, roof tiles and gutters, allowing for at least a season's growth (30–60cm). Remove most of the flowering growth from spring-flowering evergreen ceanothus, such as *Ceanothus* 'Burkwoodii' and *C. impressus*, that have finished flowering.

## DISEASE WATCH!

**Rhododendron bud blast** If you notice that your rhododendron doesn't seem to be flowering very well, take a closer look at the buds. It may be that they have become infected with a fungal disease called bud blast. The best way of avoiding the same problem occurring next year is to pick off any of the grey, furry buds that you find and throw them in the bin.

# Your garden in May

**Deadhead flowers** Remove faded flowers from pansies and violas to prolong flowering. Deadhead azaleas, rhododendrons, camellias, irises and tulips so they can put their energy into next year's display.

**Protect plants from slugs and snails** Delphiniums, hostas, strawberries and lettuces are particularly vulnerable. Pick off and destroy any that you find or see page 40.

**Take cuttings** from perennials such as Michaelmas daisies and other perennial asters, delphiniums and penstemons. Use the new shoots at the base of plants when they have reached 5–10cm.

**Tie in sweet peas** While sweet peas are getting established, they'll need to be tied to their supports. It won't be long before they start sending out tendrils, which will wrap around the support and help them climb without any further assistance.

**Tie in clematis** Clematis will head straight for the sky if you allow it, leaving you craning your neck to see the blooms at the top of the plant. The best idea is to tie the shoots so they are horizontal on their support. This will encourage them to produce flowers lower down and also keeps the plants looking neat and tidy.

**Cut back penstemon** Unlike many perennials, it's best to wait until May before cutting back last year's growth on penstemons. This is so the new growth that the pruning encourages is less likely to be damaged by the cold.

**Check soil pH** To check your soil is suitable for acid-lovers such as azaleas and rhododendrons, buy a simple pH test kit (about £1). If your soil isn't right, grow them in containers using ericaceous compost instead. Peat-free gardeners should add a handful of sulphur chips.

# 5 MINUTE JOBS

**Tie in any new shoots of climbers and wall shrubs.** Train some rose branches horizontally to encourage more flowers.

**Pinch out the growing tips** of garden chrysanthemums and dahlias to encourage branching and flowers.

**Once they're in your garden, it can be hard to persuade some plants to leave!** Forget-me-nots are one of these. To stop them becoming a pest, pull up plants as soon as they finish flowering so they don't get a chance to spread by releasing their seeds.

## IN THE GREENHOUSE

### Must-do jobs

**Shade glass** Stop your greenhouse overheating by keeping the windows and doors open. You should also shade it by either applying a temporary white paint on the outside, or shade netting on the inside. Both techniques are equally effective. Soaking the floor with water also has a cooling effect – and raises humidity, which your plants will enjoy.

**Get watering** Check your plants each morning to see if they need watering. The best technique is to stick your finger into the compost and rub it at the base of your thumb where the skin is sensitive. If it feels damp, don't water and if it feels dry, give it a good soak. It's best to water in the morning as excess water in the evening tends to hang around and can lead to problems with rots and mould.

**Plant up a hanging basket** Create a brilliant summer display by planting up a hanging basket early in May. Grown on in a greenhouse, the plants will have plenty of time to establish before going outdoors later in the month.

* Conical hanging baskets produce the best results because they offer a greater depth of compost. Place them in a deep pot so they stand up while you plant them (1).

* Pierce the basket liner to aid drainage. Fill with a container compost. Then mix some water-retaining gel and slow-release fertiliser into the compost (2).

* Fill the basket with plants, water well and then hang up in the greenhouse until all risk of frost has passed (3).

## Good to get done

**Check greenhouse temperatures** Keep an eye on how hot and cold your greenhouse is getting by using a maximum/minimum thermometer. You may be surprised by the extremes you find. It's useful to know as then you can make sure you're ventilating or insulating the greenhouse accordingly.

**Take cuttings** Many greenhouse plants will have produced plenty of fresh new growth, such as this scented pelargonium, which makes perfect material for cuttings. Select shoots without flowers and cut beneath a pair of leaves. Remove the bottom pairs of leaves and insert into a pot of compost. Water cuttings well and either put in a propagator or a plastic bag. Check regularly to see if they have made roots and move them into individual pots when their roots are growing strongly.

**Repot greenhouse tomatoes when they outgrow their pots.** Pinch out sideshoots – these can then be treated as cuttings and thereby give you more tomato plants for free. Wind the main stem around the support and tie it in if necessary. Put them into pots of free-draining compost, water in and keep in the greenhouse until they root. Alternatively, look out for plants in the garden centre.

### Still time to ...

🌿 ... **sow herbs**. Herbs that you use a lot of such as basil and parsley can be sown every couple of weeks to give you a continuous supply.

## IN THE FRUIT GARDEN

**Codling moth** There are few things more disgusting than finding a maggot in an apple. To help stop this happening, hang up a codling moth trap in your apple tree and leave it in place until August. The trap is an open-sided box that has a sticky sheet inside. A pheromone pellet is placed in the middle and attracts male moths into the trap. By checking the trap regularly and counting the number of moths found, you can time when would be most effective to spray for codling moth.

**Gooseberry sawfly larvae** These can be found on white and redcurrants as well as gooseberries. Pick off and squash any that you find.

### Good to get done

**Remove excess raspberry suckers** Raspberries can easily swamp the fruit garden if left uncontrolled, producing suckers that spread underground. Watch out for these emerging and remove any that you don't want. Raspberry plants should be about 45cm apart, so remove any excess suckers in the rows as well.

**Avoid using pesticides** when plants are in flower or you could kill beneficial insects such as bees.

### Must-do jobs

**Net soft fruit** Cover ripening fruit, such as strawberries, before the birds get there first. Make sure the netting is well secured to stop cats and other animals getting tangled up in it, as it can prove fatal for them.

**Mulch strawberry plants** If you haven't already done so, mulch strawberry plants with straw (pet shops are a good source) to keep the fruits off the ground, retain moisture and suppress weeds. It also protects the strawberries from getting splashed by mud when it rains.

# ON THE VEG PATCH

## Must-do jobs

### Sow outdoors

* Runner beans, climbing French beans and sweetcorn (if you didn't start it off indoors last month)
* Peas and dwarf beans to follow on from earlier sowings
* Maincrop carrots, swede and winter turnip (if you didn't sow them last month)
* Quick crops: beetroot, carrot, lettuce, turnip, radish, rocket, spring onion, spinach and chard, pak choi and other oriental greens

### Plant outdoors

* Brussels sprouts
* Courgettes and cucumbers
* French and runner beans
* Leeks
* Squash
* Sweetcorn
* Tomatoes

### Plant outdoors in pots

* Winter cabbage, winter cauliflower and kale

### Harvest

* Asparagus
* Radish
* Baby salad leaves
* Oriental greens
* First new potatoes started off in pots

**Cold nights** If cold nights are predicted, be prepared to nip outside to cover any of the tender vegetable plants you have planted outdoors with some fleece.

**Plant greenhouse crops** Tomatoes, peppers, cucumbers and aubergines should be large enough to plant into their final positions. If you have greenhouse borders, this is the best place for them. Before planting, remove some of the soil and replace it with garden compost or the contents of growing bags. Give it a good soaking and let it settle before planting. Alternate tomatoes with cucumbers to prevent soil diseases. When the first flower appears on peppers and aubergines, pinch this out to encourage more fruits. Pinch out the shoot tips if the plants become too leggy to keep them neat.

## Good to get done

**Erect supports for runner beans and late peas**, ensuring they won't shade neighbouring sun-lovers.

**Plant herbs** Garden centres should have plenty of these in now. Plant up a selection for use on the barbecue. Thyme, rosemary, oregano, mint, dill, basil and chives are ideal for marinades and sauces. Rosemary stems can be used as skewers for kebabs. Many herbs originate from hot, dry climates with free-draining soil, so mix sharp grit into the soil for drainage and put in a sunny spot.

**Harvest asparagus** Asparagus should not be picked for the first two years after planting to allow it to establish. However, from its third year onwards, the spears can be cut about 2.5cm under the soil for six weeks from mid-April. For the tastiest crops, pick the spears when they are about 18cm tall.

**Plant French and runner beans** Harden off young plants before planting them outside and wait until there's no risk of a late frost in your area. This could be as early as the beginning of May in the south or as late as early June in the north. Space individual bean plants about 15cm apart, or if the supports are wider apart, plant two plants per support. If you opt to sow the seed direct in the soil, push a couple of extra seeds beside each support to allow for

casualties to slugs, snails, mice or rabbits. When you plant out dwarf beans started in pots, sow a second batch alongside at the same time. These should crop three to four weeks later and nicely spread the harvest period.

**Plant out sweetcorn** Always plant sweetcorn in blocks of at least 12 plants (e.g. four rows of three) as sweetcorn is wind-pollinated. The female flowers (which eventually form the cobs) are pollinated by the male tassels at the top of the plant. You can help by shaking the plants on a still evening when the tassels are fully developed and you'll see clouds of pollen being released.

**5 MINUTE JOB**

**Twine the lead shoots** of French and runner beans the canes. Make sure you follow their natural direction and tie them in if necessary.

99

**Plant courgettes and squash** Courgettes, summer and winter squash, and marrows are not only sensitive to late frosts, but the large leaves can be damaged by wind. Harden off the plants and wait until no frosts are predicted before planting outside. In colder areas, cover the plants with fleece or cloches to shelter them from cold winds.

## PEST WATCH!

**Slugs** It's all very well protecting individual plants or sowings using barriers or slug pellets, but if you want to reduce the population once and for all, act now (see page 40).

Give each plant a good start by digging a hole about 30cm deep and wide, and filling with a mixture of soil and garden compost. This will leave a mound to plant into. On heavy or wet soils, the mound will help keep the base of the plant dry and prevent rots.

Butternuts and other winter squash can be rampant trailers. Keep them relatively neat by training the main shoots in a circle. Alternatively, plant next to sweetcorn and let the squash use the space under the corn stems.

## 5 MINUTE JOB

**To make watering courgettes easier,** cut the bottom off a plastic drink bottle, drill a small hole in the lid and half-bury it next to the plant. Then simply top up with water every now and then and each plant has its own trickle irrigation.

**Plant outdoor tomatoes and cucumbers** If you haven't got a greenhouse, plant tomatoes and cucumbers outside, after hardening off. Wait until early June in colder areas. Follow the watering tip for courgettes and squash (below opposite).

### Still time to ...

❋ **... thin seedlings**. Check the back of the seed packet and thin seedlings to the recommended spacing once they are large enough to handle. This will reduce competition and produce the best-sized crops.

❋ **... keep catch cropping** (see page 57). Any spare patch of soil can be used and if you choose the right crops, you can be picking within three to six weeks.

**Sow and plant winter crops** It seems early to be thinking about Christmas dinner, but if you want a good crop of Brussels sprouts, plant them now. As they are slow growing and greedy crops, give them plenty of space, about 90cm apart each way.

**Winter cabbage and cauliflower** can be started in pots, in a sheltered spot outdoors. Cover with fleece or netting to prevent cabbage root fly and other pests.

**Transplant leeks** Plant young plants started in trays or modules temporarily close together. Some can be pulled early as 'baby leeks' in late summer or transplanted again, following the shallots and garlic, into their final position to bulk up for winter.

## PEST WATCH!

**Blackfly on broad beans** Squash them or spray with a pesticide that contains bifenthrin.

**Brassica pests** Cover calabrese, cauliflowers and winter brassicas with a fine insect-proof mesh to prevent aphids, cabbage root fly, whitefly, caterpillars and pigeons from attacking your crops. Check there are no gaps where butterflies can sneak in. Support the net to prevent them laying their eggs through it onto leaves.

**Inter-cropping** There's plenty of scope for inter-cropping between young Brussels sprout plants. To make the most of the space available, choose a related crop to maintain the crop rotation – radish, turnip, rocket, oriental greens or even calabrese are all suitable.

# LAWNS

## Must-do jobs

**Mow the lawn** The warmer weather means that the grass cutting season is well and truly with us again. It really is worth the bother of mowing lawns once a week, as this will keep the length of the grass under control. It's much more work to battle longer grass that has been allowed to grow between infrequent mowings.

## Good to get done

**Get your lawn shipshape** Get your lawn in shape for summer by treating problems such as weeds and moss now. Spot weeders are good if you have a few patches of weeds, or else look for complete lawn carers that feed as well as weed. Also think of reseeding any bare patches (see left).

**Use lawn clippings to mulch borders** to suppress weeds and conserve moisture.

# PONDS

## Good to get done

**Plant water lilies** As the water starts to warm up, now's a good time to introduce new water lilies to your pond. To help them establish quickly and flower sooner, we recommend the following approach:

※ Pick a variety suitable for the size of your pond.
※ If your pond is large and you want to plant your lily further than you can reach, avoid getting your feet wet (if your submerged bricks are already in place) by suspending the plant in its pot from a sturdy pole and sliding it along. Lower the plant to half its required depth by standing it on submerged bricks.
※ Lower the plant each month by removing a brick until it reaches the appropriate depth.

## HOW TO PLANT A SUMMER CONTAINER

Replanting your containers can be costly and time consuming, but by choosing a few permanent structural plants and leaving space for seasonal colour, there's really no need to replace all your container plants and compost every few months. In this container, for example, there are a couple of variegated ivies and a topiary pyramid box. These evergreen plants will last the year round and will look different each time the container is re-planted – and it means you have fewer plants to buy for each new season.

**1** Paint a wooden container in a summery coat of emulsion.

### WHAT YOU WILL NEED

❀ Container compost
❀ Slow-release fertiliser
❀ Water-retaining gel
❀ 1 x topiary pyramid box
❀ 2 x 9cm variegated ivies
❀ 2 x sugar-almond plant
❀ 3 x million bells
❀ 1 x mercadonia
❀ 1 x thyme
❀ 1 x verbena
❀ 4 x angelonia

**2** Remove any plants that you planted in earlier in the year and some of the old compost, which can be replanted in the garden.

**3** Refresh the container by adding some new compost along with slow-release fertiliser and water-retaining gel.

**4** Decide on the arrangement of your plants before planting and then top up with more compost. Water thoroughly.

**5** Unlike plants in the garden, plants in containers are reliant on you for all their food and water. Water them regularly and thoroughly using a watering can with the rose removed. An occasional liquid feed will give plants a boost and regular removal of faded blooms will ensure a long flowering season. Furthermore, deadheading will keep the plants looking neat and in good shape.

# YOUR GARDEN IN JUNE

June is the perfect month for instantly livening up your borders with colourful bedding plants. Other important jobs for this month include deadheading roses, moving baskets and pots outdoors, training tomatoes, thinning out fruit and getting strawberry plants for free.

# TOP JOBS THIS MONTH

 **BORDERS**

Plant bedding
Cut back oriental poppies
Move baskets and pots outdoors
Deadhead roses
Water and feed new plants and pots
Fill gaps
Mulch borders
Deadhead flowers
Pick sweet peas
Continue to stake those tall and floppy plants that continue to grow
Clip box plants

 **IN THE GREENHOUSE**

Train tomatoes
Sow seeds
Keep things cool
Control whitefly

 **IN THE FRUIT GARDEN**

Thin out fruit
Pick soft fruit
Encourage strawberry runners

 **ON THE VEG PATCH**

Continue to sow more catch crops
Sow late crops
Feed crops
Keep weeds down
Harvest salads, peas and early crops
Earth up your potatoes

 **LAWNS**

Mow regularly
Treat slow-growing weeds

**PONDS**

Remove pond weed

## BORDERS

### Must-do jobs

**Plant bedding** The risk of frost has largely passed so it's now safe to start planting out your bedding. If you haven't grown your own, you'll find a good selection of annuals and tender perennials for sale at the garden centre – try, too, to get the most recent delivery that's looking fresh and green with plenty of buds. Don't delay as the best will quickly sell out. Plant them at the spacing recommended on the label (or seed packet if you've grown your own). Remember to keep plants well watered for the first month or so while they're putting down new roots and make sure you protect them from slugs and snails while they're settling in.

### Still time to ...

✿ ... **prune spring-flowering shrubs**. Shrubs that flower in late spring such as weigela, flowering currant, philadelphus, forsythia, broom and deutzia should be pruned as soon as blooms fade – see page 67.

✿ ... **tidy bulb foliage**. Don't get your secateurs out until the foliage of bulbs such as daffodils and tulips has turned yellow or you may miss out on flowers next year (see page 71).

✿ ... **create a wonderful plant-filled patio** by arranging hanging baskets and containers (see pages 94 and 104).

**Cut back oriental poppies** when they've finished blooming. This will encourage fresh foliage and may even reward you with some extra blooms. Cut the whole plant back to ground level to stop it collapsing in a messy heap. New growth will follow shortly and should even produce an extra show of flowers later in the season.

**Move baskets and pots outdoors** Check that brackets are firmly attached to the wall before hanging up your baskets. If you didn't get a chance to plant containers earlier in the year, don't despair, as many garden centres offer ready-planted ones. When selecting yours, don't be swayed by colourful displays, instead look for ones with lots of flowerbuds that will produce a good show in the coming weeks.

**Deadhead roses** June sees the main flush of rose flowers. Many old-fashioned varieties only bloom this month but modern ones will go on all summer. To put their energy into flowers instead of seeds, cut off the old blooms as soon as they fade. Don't just tweak off the older blooms as they fade, use secateurs to cut back to above a leaf that points in the direction you want the new shoot to grow.

**PEST WATCH!**

**Aphids** These small sap-sucking pests rapidly multiply at this time of year. They not only weaken the plant but can also spread viruses. Squash any you find or spray with a suitable pesticide (see page 70).

**Lily beetles** These continue to be a problem (also see page 70).

**Vine weevil larvae** Adult beetles will soon start appearing to look for places to lay their eggs (see page 88).

## Good to get done

**Water and feed** It's worth regularly watering anything that you have recently planted in your borders to help them become established, as well as your pots, planters and hanging baskets. Unless you added slow-release fertiliser to the compost when planting your baskets and containers, start feeding them now with a liquid feed.

**Fill gaps** Unexpected gaps often appear at this time of year and if you don't fill them quickly, they'll become more obvious as summer progresses. Summer-flowering bedding will give instant colour, although you've still got time to fill larger holes by sowing annuals directly in the soil. Alternatively, you can also plant perennials and shrubs (see page 160), but you'll need to keep them well watered.

**Mulch your borders** with composted bark or garden compost. It helps keep them moist and suppresses weeds, so you won't have to water or weed them so often. Ensure you don't dig mulch in.

**Plant herbs in a pot** Plant up a container with your favourite herbs, such as basil, chives, sage, tarragon and parsley, and keep it close to your barbecue so they're at hand when you need them. By keeping herbs watered and fed, a container should be able to keep you going all summer.

**Deadhead basket and container flowers** Encourage your basket and container plants to flower more freely, and for longer, by removing blooms as they fade. It'll stop your plants producing seed and wasting energy that's better spent on more flowers.

**Pick sweet peas** Sweet peas are one of the highlights of early summer. They could never be accused of being mean with their flowers as they produce more and more every time you cut some. In fact, if you don't pick them, the plant will stop blooming, thinking that it has done its job of making seeds for next year's plants. It is worth squashing any greenfly that you find as they can spread sweet pea virus, which will also bring a premature halt to your displays.

**Continue to stake plants** Support tall and floppy plants with funnels, loops, Y-stakes, rings, border restraints or spirals before they get out of control. Alternatively, use pea sticks, netting and canes.

**Clip box plants** Box hedges and topiary can start to look a bit shaggy once new growth appears. Give them a quick trim now to keep them in shape. If your plant needs something more drastic than a simple haircut, it will respond well to being cut back hard if you feed and mulch it afterwards.

**Water containers** Check containers daily and water if the compost feels dry to the touch. If you used slow-release fertiliser when planting, you won't need to give additional liquid feed yet. To keep plants flowering, remove the old blooms as they fade.

**Stop euphorbia spreading** Euphorbia seedlings will spring up all over your garden if you don't remove the flower heads at the base when they fade. Always wear gloves when handling euphorbia as the milky sap can irritate skin.

# 5 MINUTE JOB

**Cut back aubretia** Give this pretty spring flower a drastic haircut now to stop plants from becoming straggly and unkempt.

# IN THE GREENHOUSE

## Must-do jobs

**Train tomatoes** Tomatoes, both indoors and out, will be growing strongly. If you have cordon varieties, they need to be trained to have one central stem to channel the plant's energy into producing the fruit. To do this, simply remove any sideshoots that appear between the central stem and the leaves. Then tie the plants into their supports. For the best crops, also feed them regularly with a tomato feed when you water.

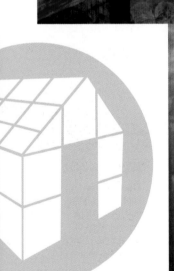

**Plant greenhouse tomatoes, cucumbers, peppers and aubergines into their final pots** or in the greenhouse border if you haven't already done so.

## Good to get done

**Sow seeds** Biennials, such as foxgloves and wallflowers, are sown one year to flower the next. It's tempting to wait until autumn and buy them as plants, but for the best selection of varieties, it's worth sowing some from seed. A border

filled with pure-white foxgloves is a real head-turner. You can also sow Brompton stocks, honesty, primulas, violas and winter-flowering pansies under glass now. Keep sowings in pots and trays in the shade and don't let the temperature reach over 18°C as this can inhibit germination (see also pages 60–1).

**Keep things cool**
Open the vents and greenhouse door first thing on warm days to keep temperatures down. It will also encourage air flow, which helps prevent fungal diseases.

# 5 MINUTE JOB

**Control whitefly** and other flying pests with yellow sticky traps. Hang them on wires near your plants for chemical-free insect control.

# IN THE FRUIT GARDEN

## Must-do jobs

**Thin out fruit** Fruit trees tend to produce a lot of young fruits. If they were all to develop, the fruit would end up small and misshapen because the tree can't provide them with enough nutrients to enable them all to grow properly.

A certain number naturally fall off – it's called 'June drop' – but you still need to thin them further. Reduce the number of fruits on your trees so that those left are the following distances apart:

* Cooking apples: 15–22cm
* Dessert apples: 10–15cm
* Peaches: 15–20cm
* Pears: 10–15cm
* Plums: 8–10cm

## Good to get done

### Pick soft fruit

Strawberries, raspberries and hybrid berries are all starting to produce tempting crops that should be ready to harvest now. If you haven't already covered your plants with netting to keep out scavengers, do it quickly before the birds get there first.

**Get strawberry plants for free** Strawberry plants naturally spread by producing runners – new small plants that grow on the end of a long sideshoot. Grow these on and you'll have plenty of new plants laden with fruit next year. Here's how to do it:

❋ When you find a runner, dig a small hole in the soil where it lies. Place a small pot filled with multipurpose compost into the hole. The hole should ensure that your pot stays upright.

❋ Push the young plant into the surface of the compost and secure it using a peg or staple – a piece of bent wire is fine.

❋ Keep the new plant well watered and as soon as it starts to grow, cut the stem that connects it to its parent. You can now move your new strawberry plant to a sunny spot and grow it on.

## 5 MINUTE JOB

**Tie in berries** Berries such as blackberries and tayberries produce their fruit on growth produced the previous year. This makes it easy to train and prune them. Simply tie new growth in the opposite direction to the growth that is fruiting.

# ON THE VEG PATCH

## Must-do jobs

### Sow outdoors

✤ Catch crops: beetroot, carrot, radish, spring onion, lettuce, baby salad leaf, turnip, Chinese cabbage, pak choi and other oriental greens
✤ Late crops: peas, dwarf beans, calabrese, leaf beet

### Plant outdoors

✤ Celery and celeriac

### Harvest

✤ New potatoes
✤ Peas and mangetout
✤ Broad beans
✤ Spinach and leaf beet
✤ Lettuce and salad leaves
✤ Radish
✤ Carrots and courgettes

**Tender crops** In colder areas, if your plot is prone to late frosts or if the weather hasn't been favourable during May, there's still time to plant out tender crops, such as courgettes, squash and marrow, sweetcorn and French and runner beans.

**Feed crops** At this point in the season, scatter a balanced fertiliser around greedier crops. Larger brassicas, maincrop potatoes and chard would all benefit. Peas and beans, onions and carrots generally don't require extra nutrients.

**Keep weeds down** It's not just your crops that are growing like mad now. Weed seedlings in the soil will rapidly take over if you let them. Larger, leafy crops will eventually shade out weeds, but don't need the competition when they are getting established.

## DISEASE WATCH!

**Brassica downy mildew** Remove any yellowing leaves on brassicas to stop this disease spreading (see page 56).

# Your garden in June

## PEST WATCH!

**Asparagus beetle**
Watch out for the adults and greyish-black grubs which feed on asparagus stems and bark, which can cause the foliage and stems to die. Remove any you find by hand or spray with organic insect killer.

**Blackfly on runner beans** Netting is not an option – apart from the height, runner beans need pollinating insects. Spray a couple of times with a soft soap or pyrethrum-based insecticide in the evening to avoid harming bees, or rub off any colonies that appear.

## Good to get done

**Give courgettes a helping hand** If the weather has been cold and not much fruit has set on your courgette plants, then you can give them a helping hand by fertilising the flowers. To do this, find a male flower (without a swelling behind it), remove the petals and push it into a female flower, which can be identified by the swelling behind it.

**Harvest salad** Snip a few leaves as soon as they're big enough to eat. They should resprout in a week or so, giving you more crops. If you leave them without cutting, plants are likely to produce flowers and will need to be pulled up.

**Harvest peas and broad beans** Unless you have a patch of asparagus, peas and beans are likely to be your first real crops. The trick with both crops is to spread the harvest by picking early and regularly to avoid a glut. The worst that can happen is that you end up freezing the surplus to enjoy later in the year.

**Harvest other early crops** Any veg started in pots in the greenhouse should be cropping by now, including early potatoes, carrots and courgettes. Use these before starting on the first outdoor crops. Early in the season you may need to harvest potatoes from two or more plants to get enough for a meal, but the remaining plants will soon bulk up. Instead of digging up a potato plant, push your hand into the side of the ridge and feel

around for any tubers the size of a hen's egg. Leave smaller ones and replace the soil.

**Fill gaps** Sometimes holes appear unexpectedly in your planting plan. Fortunately, garden centres usually have plenty of plants to fill the gaps, though you may have little choice of variety. Even at this stage it's worth sowing extra seed to fill these gaps – the replacements will soon catch up with earlier sowings. If the soil is dry, give it a good soaking before sowing.

## PEST WATCH!

**Cabbage white caterpillars** Look out for tell-tale holes on cabbage leaves and if you find any of the caterpillars, pick them off. The only sure way to control them is to prevent the female butterflies laying their eggs and this means keeping the fine mesh covers in place. Check regularly that there are no gaps and that the crop isn't touching the net – they will squeeze through the smallest gap and lay eggs through the mesh. If any do get through, spray with a contact insecticide or squash them by hand.

## Still time to ...

✿ **... plant tender veg outdoors**. If you haven't sown tender veg, such as squash and sweetcorn from seed, you can buy plants from the garden centre.

✿ **... earth up potatoes**. Earth up your potatoes to stop spuds turning green in the light and protect them from the cold (see page 78).

✿ **... plant winter crops** (see page 101).

**Plant out celery and celeriac** These plants should be large enough to plant out now. Self-blanching varieties should be planted in blocks, but this isn't essential for green types such as 'Victoria'.

**Ensure water reaches roots** When you're planting in dry conditions, make a slight depression for each plant and soak the soil a couple of hours before planting. The depression will allow you to water the plants without wasting water on the surrounding soil.

# LAWNS

## Must-do jobs

**Mow your lawn every week** It will soon thicken up, becoming dense and more wear-resistant. This will also prevent any weeds in it flowering and setting seed, and so will stop them from spreading.

**Treat slow-growing weeds** Go over your lawn with a spring-tine rake before you mow. This lifts up low, creeping weeds like clover and yarrow so that they get caught in the mower blades.

## Good to get done

**Neaten the edges** If you haven't got time to mow the lawn, simply do the edges with an electric trimmer. It'll keep it looking tidy until you have time to mow it properly.

**Feed grass** Grass quickly responds to feeding by turning a darker shade of green. Remember to water new lawns in dry spells.

# PONDS

## Good to get done

**Remove pond weed** Submerged pond plants need clear water so that sunlight can reach them. Unfortunately, floating plants like duckweed grow quickly and block out the light, causing other plants and pond life to die. There are no chemical controls, so scoop out as much as possible using a net, sieve or bowl.

## PEST WATCH!

**Water lily aphids** attack many types of pond plant. You can't use insecticides near a pond so just blast them off your plants using a hosepipe. The pond predators will do the rest.

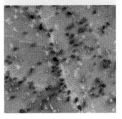

## WHAT YOU WILL NEED

- 2 x non-porous glazed containers, one much smaller in diameter than the other as it will sit on top
- Small fountain pump
- Large plastic pot to fit inside the large container
- Small plastic plant pot to fit inside the small container
- Silicone sealant and gun
- 45cm-length of 13mm-diameter flexible pipe
- Heavy-duty galvanized mesh to fit inside the top of each container
- Fine plastic mesh to fit inside the top of each container
- 1 x bag of polished pebbles
- Scissors
- Wire cutters or pliers
- Stanley knife

# HOW TO MAKE A WATER FEATURE

This simple, freestanding water feature is an easy way to bring a splash to your garden. We put ours in dappled shade, surrounded by potted Japanese maples and hostas, but it would be just as effective anywhere in the garden.

**1** Thread the lead from the pump through the drainage hole in the large container, leaving plenty of slack to allow for lifting the pump out for maintenance. Seal with silicone sealant. Leave for 24 hours to set.

**2** Cut out the base of the large plastic pot and place in the large container with the pump in the middle. The top of the pot should sit 5cm below the top of the container to allow for mesh and pebbles.

**3** Trim the mesh to slightly less than the diameter of the large container so it will sit on top of the plastic pot inside. Fit the flexible pipe to the pump and feed it through the mesh.

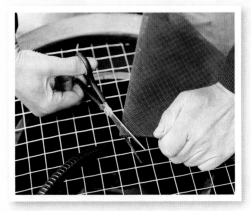

**4** Cut a piece of fine plastic mesh to sit on top of the galvanized mesh and cut a central hole for the pipe. This fine mesh will stop pebbles and debris falling through.

**5** Feed the pipe through the base of the smaller container. Trim the pipe to 1–2cm above the rim of the small container. Repeat steps 2–4 with the small plastic pot.

**6** Fill the larger container with water, do a test run and adjust the length of the flexible pipe as necessary. Cover the mesh with pebbles, switch on, and enjoy!

# YOUR GARDEN IN JULY

This is a brilliant time of year to enjoy your garden – there will be fruit ready to pick, plenty of flowers in bloom, shrubs that will have grown enormously and so can now be given a neat trim, and plenty of home-grown veg ready to fill your dinner plate.

# TOP JOBS THIS MONTH

## BORDERS
Keep patio displays looking good
Feed your roses
Provide water for wildlife
Trim hedges, checking for nesting birds
Pot up or move self-seeding plants
Water only if needed
Try to use water butts
Prune pyracantha
Look out for bargains being sold at garden centres
Organise watering of pots if you are going on holiday

## IN THE GREENHOUSE
Keep growing bags watered
Take lavender cuttings
Look out for red spider mite

## IN THE FRUIT GARDEN
Pick summer fruit
Rake up fallen leaves

## ON THE VEG PATCH
Sow beans and spring cabbage outdoors
Sow more quick crops
Plant for the winter
Water thoroughly just once a week
Pick crops
Plant second crops

## LAWNS
Allow your grass to grow longer
Cut the lawn at least once a week

## PONDS
Remove plant debris

## BORDERS

### Must-do jobs

**Keep patio displays looking good** Make sure that hanging baskets and patio containers are a blaze of colour until the first frosts. Touch the compost every morning and water thoroughly if it feels dry. In hot weather, it's worth checking more than once a day. Feed plants weekly with a soluble feed and cut flowers as soon as they fade. If you're going away for a few days, soak them thoroughly and stand them in a shady corner.

### Still time to ...

❀ **... stake tall plants.** Tie in tall or floppy plants to stop them looking untidy and prevent them snapping in the wind and rain.

**Feed your roses** As roses are heavy feeders it's good to feed them in midsummer as well as in March. This will help encourage a second flush of flowers.

**Provide water for wildlife** Summer can be a thirsty time for garden wildlife so refill your birdbaths and bowls with fresh water every day. Forget too often and you'll find that birds can be quite unforgiving. If they can't wet their whistle when they need to in your garden, they'll stop coming. Also, to prevent the build-up of diseases, wash your water bowls out at least once every two weeks.

## Good to get done

**Trim hedges** July and August are key months to trim hedges, which keeps them neat and restricts their growth. The pieces of equipment to use are cordless or mains hedge trimmers or hedging shears. The growth rate slows down in autumn so your hedges will stay looking neat until the following year. Before starting, always check for any nesting birds.

❋ When pruning hedges planted with small-leafed shrubs, like privet (*Ligustrum ovalifolium*) and shrubby honeysuckle (*Lonicera nitida*), you'll get the best finish by using shears or a hedge trimmer.

❋ When pruning hedges planted with large-leafed shrubs, such as holly (*Ilex aquifolium*) and laurel (*Prunus laurocerasus*), use secateurs. If you use this tool instead of shears, you can neatly cut the stems without leaving tattered foliage.

**Look out for self-seeding plants**
Many perennials seed themselves freely around the garden, so keep an eye out. You can easily pot up or move any young plants you find and move them to other parts of the garden.

131

## PEST WATCH!

**Earwigs** Earwigs will shred dahlia flowers. To prevent damage, put a few flowerpots stuffed with straw upside-down on sticks among your dahlias and empty them out each morning so you can kill any earwigs you find.

**Water only if needed** If the weather's dry, don't panic and water everything. Established plants should be fine, as will lawns, which will quickly turn green again once the rain returns. Anything that's been planted in the last month or so will need help. It's better to give plants a drench once a week rather than a sprinkle every day or you'll encourage shallow roots that are vulnerable to drying out. Try to use water butts or grey water where possible and watch out for hosepipe bans in your area.

**Prune pyracantha** Pyracantha flowers and fruits on wood produced the previous year. To reveal the berries and encourage a good display next year on wall-trained shrubs, cut back the sideshoots to two to three leaves from their base. The stems of pyracantha are very thorny so wear gloves.

**Look out for bargains** After the spring rush, many garden centres offer summer sales as a way of tempting us back through their doors. It can be a great chance to pick up good bargains on plants, pots and furniture in particular, as garden centres try to clear the stock that they didn't sell earlier in spring.

## Still time to ...

✿ **... tie in climbers** (see pages 92–3). Climbers flower best when their stems are trained horizontally. If you allow them to grow straight up, the blooms will be tantalisingly out of sight above your head. Check on them regularly and tie in new growth while it's still flexible.

**Cut back hardy geraniums** Many early flowering perennials that have finished blooming can look very tatty during July. The best thing to do is to cut them back hard. This encourages the plants to produce new foliage, and even a second flush of flowers. Our past research has found this technique particularly effective with Lady's mantle (*alchemilla*), catmint (*nepeta*), hardy geraniums and oriental poppies (*Papaver orientalis*).

# IN THE GREENHOUSE

## Must-do jobs

**Keep growing bags watered** Growing bags can quickly dry out in warm weather because the compost has little depth. Check them daily and water when necessary.

### PEST WATCH!

**Red spider mite** can be a real nuisance in the greenhouse and attack any plant, sucking its sap and seriously weakening it. The mites spread very quickly, so look out for mottled foliage and tiny webs on the undersides of the leaves. Spray your plants as soon as you see these symptoms with an insecticide containing bifenthrin or use a biological control.

## Good to get done

**Take lavender cuttings** Lavender is a garden favourite and as it's easy to grow from cuttings, you can easily have all the plants you'll ever need.

🌸 Use a sharp knife and cut off a healthy looking shoot that's roughly 10cm long.

🌸 Pull some of the leaves off the lower 5cm of stem.

🌸 Insert the cuttings into pots containing a mixture of 50/50 multipurpose compost and sharp sand.

🌸 Water them lightly and place them in a cool, shady corner in the greenhouse, where they'll root in a few weeks. You can then plant them outside in spring.

# Your garden in July

## IN THE FRUIT GARDEN

### Must-do jobs

**Time for sticky fingers** Picking summer fruit is a pleasure and there's certainly plenty to look forward to in July and August. The following crops should all be ready to pick now: early plums; blackberries; black, red and white currants; gooseberries; raspberries and blueberries. Pick them as soon as they're ripe as there are plenty of pests and hungry wildlife that'll take advantage.

**Rake up fallen leaves** Fruit trees are prone to many fungal diseases such as mildew, rust, scab and silver leaf. The spores of these diseases are often carried on the foliage. To help prevent your trees being attacked next year, rake up any fallen leaves and fruit, and either burn them or throw them in the bin.

### Good to get done

**Prune trained apples and pears** Trained fruit such as apple cordons, plum pyramids, and fans should be pruned in summer to keep them in their allotted space.

🌸 On apples and pears, the new growth becomes woody at the base, cut back sideshoots that come directly from the main stems to three leaves from the base.

🌸 Cut back any that come from spurs or existing sideshoots to one leaf from the base. Completely remove any vigorous, upright shoots.

🌸 On pyramid plums, cut back new shoots on main stems to 20cm and sideshoots to 15cm.

🌸 On fan-trained plums, cut non-essential new shoots to three leaves after fruiting.

# ON THE VEG PATCH

## Must-do jobs

### Sow outdoors
❀ Dwarf French beans
❀ Late runner beans
❀ Spring cabbage
❀ Quick crops: beetroot, carrots, lettuce, salad leaves, oriental greens, spring onion, radish, turnip, spinach

### Plant outdoors
❀ Leeks
❀ Winter brassicas

### Harvest
❀ Last peas and broad beans
❀ Dwarf, climbing and runner beans
❀ Baby beets, baby carrots, radish, spring onion
❀ Garlic and shallots
❀ Second early potatoes
❀ Courgettes
❀ Calabrese
❀ Spinach and chard

**Water sensibly** If it's a hot, dry summer, concentrate water on the following crops:
❀ Quick-growing leafy salads
❀ Cauliflowers and calabrese as they start to produce heads
❀ Beans, including runners, that are in flower
❀ Seedlings and newly planted veg until they are established

**Give individual crops a really thorough soaking** once a week or fortnight rather than trying to keep the whole plot watered on a daily basis.

**Blight** The fungal disease blight has devastated potato and tomato crops in the last few years during spells of warm, wet weather. Watch out for the first signs of black patches on the foliage and cut off the stems of infected plants. It's best to either bin or burn them – don't put them in your compost heap as doing so will keep the disease spores in your garden, which could spread to next year's crop. Potatoes underground should be fine to use but wait a couple of weeks before digging up to let the blight spores on the surface die. Unfortunately, affected tomatoes either tend to rot on the plant or a few days after picking.

**Plant for winter** If you haven't raised your own plants already from seed (see pages 60–1), you can easily buy them from garden centres as young plants. When planting them, cover them with a protective fleece to safeguard them from insect pests.

## Good to get done

**Pick courgettes** as soon as they reach 15cm long (or pick when they're shorter if you're facing a glut). If you want the flowers for stuffing, pick them early in the morning and keep them in the fridge. Use the male flowers (which haven't got a swelling at their base) but use the female ones as well if you've got a glut of fruits!

**Start pulling carrots and beetroots** as soon as they're large enough (1cm across the top for carrots and 2.5cm for baby beets). Try not to disturb neighbouring roots and leave these to grow on.

**Harvest potoatoes** When you've dug the last of the early potatoes, start on the second earlies. The second early varieties should keep going until the autumn when the maincrop varieties are ready to be dug up and stored in a cool, dry place for winter. If the tubers start to get too big before you need them, cut off the tops and leave them in the ground until you want them. This will also help prevent blight spoiling them (see box, opposite). Remove as many tubers as you can, even the smallest. 'Volunteer' potatoes always seem to pop up where you least want them the following year. They can also carry blight.

**Plant winter brassicas** Harvest any remaining catch crops and plant out winter brassicas such as savoy and winter cabbage, kale, autumn cauliflowers, Brussels sprouts, sprouting broccoli and a late sowing of calabrese. Plant next year's Brussels sprouts if you didn't do this in May. Don't loosen the soil when planting large brassicas. Firm them in well so they'll stand up against winter winds.

**Spring cabbage** For greens next spring, sow spring cabbage in a seedbed or module trays (see pages 60–1) for planting out in September. Keep the seedlings watered and protect them from pests.

**Plant second crops** As early crops are cleared, replace them immediately with a second summer crop or one for the winter. Hoe off any weeds, and scatter some general purpose fertiliser. Give the ground a thorough soaking if it's dry. The soil should be warm enough to sow tender crops direct too. Dwarf French beans are relatively quick; runner beans will be cropping prolifically by now, but it's still worth making a late sowing; and leeks can be transplanted into their final position now.

# LAWNS

## Must-do jobs

**Take extra care during hot weather** Lawns often turn yellow during dry spells and it's tempting to water them. Unfortunately, to keep them green requires a lot of water, which may not be practical. Instead, let nature takes its course and leave your grass unwatered. Although lawns die back during drought, they rarely die completely and will soon turn green again when the rain returns. Here are some tips to help your lawn look its best during dry weather:

* Allow your grass to grow longer by setting your mower blades higher. This will reduce the stress on your lawn.
* Cut the lawn at least once a week as long grass is far harder to cut.
* Leave the grass clippings on your lawn when you mow it as they will act as a mulch, helping to conserve moisture.
* Remove any obvious weeds from your lawn as these compete for moisture.

# PONDS

## Good to get done

**Remove plant debris** To help keep your pond water clear, remove spent leaves and stems from your aquatic and pond-side plants. Plant debris quickly decays in water and can affect the nutrient balance, which could mean that algae and blanket weed will grow more readily.

## Still time to ...

* **... remove weed from ponds**. Blanket weed can grow at a surprising rate (see page 81).

## HOW TO HELP YOUR CONTAINER PLANTS SURVIVE THE HOLIDAYS

Whether you're going away for a long weekend, a week or a fortnight, your container plants can be a worry. They can't cope without watering in the way that plants in your borders can. On your return, you may well be familiar with the tell-tale signs of wilting, fewer leaves and flowers, and even diseases, such as powdery mildew. So if you know that you're not always going to be around to take care of your pots in the summer months, why not choose plants that you know can cope with a bit of neglect?

### How to help your plants

**Plant them** in container compost.

**Include** slow-release fertiliser when you pot up your plants.

**Mulch your pots** with gravel or another mulch of your choosing to reduce water evaporation.

**Liquid feed** plants for an occasional boost.

**Watch** for sap-sucking pests like greenfly and treat them before they weaken plants.

**Just before** you go away, give your plants a good soak.

**Consider** an automatic watering system on a timer.

## Plants that can be left happily without care for two weeks
- Begonia
- Solenostemon (coleus)
- Gazania
- Ivy
- Pelargonium (geranium)
- Verbena

## Will revive after some neglect
- Dianthus (pink)
- Gaillardia
- Scaevola

## Will stand limited neglect
- Diascia
- Fuchsia
- Helichrysum
- Nepeta (also known as glechoma)
- Osteospermum

## Don't neglect!
- Bidens
- Lobelia
- Surfinia (petunia)

# YOUR GARDEN IN AUGUST

Summer has arrived! No matter how good or bad the weather, there are loads of jobs to do. During the school holidays, gardening is often a family affair with seeds to collect and produce to harvest from the veg patch – all perfect jobs to do together.

# TOP JOBS THIS MONTH

##  BORDERS

Prune wisteria
Deadhead flowers
Water containers
Prune ornamental trees
Take cuttings of half-hardy plants
Deal with tough weeds
Buy bulbs
Collect seed
Look out for powdery mildew

##  IN THE GREENHOUSE

Damp down the greenhouse floor

##  IN THE FRUIT GARDEN

Prune summer-fruiting berries
Keep an eye open for brown rot
Rake up fruit that has fallen early

##  ON THE VEG PATCH

Sow late beans, spring cabbage as well as quick crops
Harvest the last of the peas and broad beans
Keep a beady eye open for cabbage white caterpillars
Lift garlic and shallots
Sow green manure

##  LAWNS

Allow your grass to grow longer
Cut the lawn at least once a week
Leave grass clippings on the lawn
Remove obvious weeds

##  PONDS

Clean the filter in a pond or water feature pump

## BORDERS

### Must-do jobs

**Prune wisteria** Pruning is one of the keys to success to encourage wisteria to flower well. All of the long whippy growth that it has made this year should either be tied into the support to cover new areas or cut back to two or three buds from old wood. Some gardeners choose to cut back in two stages, but you can avoid freezing to death up a ladder in February by doing it in one go in August.

### Still time to ...

❊ **... stake tall plants**. Tie in tall or floppy plants to stop them looking untidy and snapping in the wind and rain (see page 68).

**Deadhead flowers** Keep your floral displays going by removing flowers as soon as they fade. This stops the plant diverting its energy into seed production and, instead, it concentrates all its efforts into making new blooms.

## Good to get done

**Water containers** By August, your container displays may be beginning to flag even if you added slow-release fertiliser at planting, so give them a liquid feed to perk them up again.

**Prune ornamental trees** August is a good month to prune ornamental trees such as flowering cherries and mountain ash, as there are fewer diseases around now to infect the wounds. Pruning them at this time will also allow them to heal fully before winter. When pruning, always use sharp tools to ensure the cuts are clean. If you're removing an entire branch, make the cut good and close to the trunk, but without actually cutting into it.

❉ First, remove any damaged or diseased branches, weak growth or unwanted stems growing from the tree base.

❉ Then look for any stems and branches that cross or rub against each other, as these can be sites of infection. Remove the weakest.

❉ Finally, remove any branches that make the tree look lop-sided, or are going in the wrong direction.

## DISEASE WATCH!

**Powdery mildew**
This fungal disease is common in late summer, especially if it has been dry and hot. A white coating covers the leaves and other parts of the plant. Growth may be poor as a result but most plants recover. To reduce the risk of it happening again, mulch around plants to help trap moisture in the soil. Use an appropriate fungicide if necessary and keep plants well watered but avoid getting water on the leaves.

**Take cuttings of half-hardy plants** For any half-hardy plants you'd like to keep for next year, take a few cuttings now. They'll take up less space indoors over winter than lifting the original plant.

**Deal with tough weeds** Late summer is a good time to spray tough weeds with a weedkiller containing glyphosate as they are naturally drawing their energy back into

their roots and so are more likely to take in a lethal dose. Be careful not to spray anything you want to keep.

**Buy bulbs** It seems mad to be thinking of spring already but by August, most garden centres will have their bulb displays in place. It's a good idea to buy them sooner rather than later as you'll have the best choice of varieties and the bulbs will be in great condition. Look for autumn crocus, colchicum, sternbergia, amaryllis and nerine. Most bulbs, except tulips, can be planted straight away, but if you haven't got any space yet, store them in a dry, cool place, such as a shed. Make a note that you put them there as it's all too easy for them to lie forgotten! Plant autumn-flowering bulbs such as colchicum as soon as possible.

## 5 MINUTE JOB

**Collect seed** Collect the seed of any plants you'd like to keep for next year. Cover the seedheads with paper bags and tap out the contents. Either sow straight away or store in the fridge and wait until next spring before you use them. Remember, there's no point saving seeds from varieties with F1 in the name as their progeny is never the same as the parent.

# IN THE GREENHOUSE

### Must-do jobs

**Damp down the greenhouse floor** Keep the greenhouse cool on hot days by wetting the floor, which will help cool and humidify the air as it evaporates. It's also good to open the door, vents and windows to encourage air circulation. This has the added benefit of reducing the risk of fungal diseases, which enjoy static air.

# IN THE FRUIT GARDEN

### Must-do jobs

**Prune summer-fruiting raspberries, blackberries and hybrid berries** Cut back all the canes that have fruited this year to ground level. This is to make space for the green canes that were produced this spring and will fruit next year. Tie in new growth to the support as this will produce next year's crops.

## 5 MINUTE JOB

**Less-than-perfect fruit** will often fall from the tree early. Rake it up or it will become a magnet for wasps.

## DISEASE WATCH!

**Brown rot** It begins as a soft, brown area on the skin of tree fruits such as apples and plums, and rapidly spreads, turning the whole fruit brown. Rings of white pustules also appear. The fruits may fall off the tree, but others will hang on and dry out. Gather any you find to reduce the risk of this fungal disease spreading.

**PEST WATCH!**

**PEST WATCH!**

**Cabbage white caterpillars** The yellow and black caterpillars can swarm over plants from the brassica family, stripping their leaves horribly fast (see page 121).

## ON THE VEG PATCH

### Must-do jobs
**Sow outdoors**
- ✿ Dwarf French beans
- ✿ Late runner beans
- ✿ Spring cabbage

**Quick crops**: beetroot, carrots, lettuce, salad leaves, oriental greens, spring onion, radish, turnip, spinach

### Harvest
- ✿ Last peas and broad beans
- ✿ Dwarf, climbing and runner beans
- ✿ Baby beets, baby carrots, radish, spring onion
- ✿ Garlic and shallots
- ✿ Second early potatoes
- ✿ Courgettes
- ✿ Calabrese
- ✿ Salad
- ✿ Spinach and chard

### Good to get done
**Harvest last of the peas and broad beans** Keep picking them regularly until no more pods are produced. Cut the top growth for the compost heap, but leave the roots in the ground. The nitrogen-fixing nodules on the roots will rot to benefit the following crop.

**Lift garlic and shallots** As soon as the tops start to die off, scoop the soil from around the bulbs to expose them to sunlight and help ripen them. Once the tops have dried, lift the bulbs and leave them on the soil to dry for storage. If wet weather is predicted, lay them on trays under cover or on greenhouse shelves to dry. Store the garlic and shallots bulbs on wooden trays or in net bags in a cool, dry place for winter use.

**Uncover squash fruits** Help squash to ripen in the sun by removing any leaves, which are shading them. Squash plants grow at a remarkable rate so check for new leaves regularly.

**Sow green manure** At this time of year, you are likely to be clearing areas of ground faster than you can fill them with late or over-winter crops. There's nothing wrong with leaving bare soil, though you can make it work over winter by sowing a green manure crop, which has several advantages: nutrients left in the soil that would otherwise be flushed out by winter rain will be mopped up; the green manure will help suppress weeds; it will prevent a hard crust forming on the soil; and it will provide bulky plant material that can be dug in before the spring crops go in or added to the compost heap. Choose a hardy green manure, such as winter tares, clovers or phacelia, and sow when the soil is warm and moist. Broadcast the seed and rake it in. The following spring, chop it with a spade before it sets seed and dig it in, allowing it time to rot down before sowing spring crops.

## LAWNS

### Must-do jobs
**Keep up the good work** Continue to follow the advice given in July to help keep your lawn in tip-top condition (see page 139).

## PONDS

### Good to get done
**Clean the filter** If you have a pump in your pond or water feature, midsummer is a good time to clean it. This will keep the pump working properly and should help prolong its life. Never wash the filter with tap water as it contains chlorine that can kill bacteria that's vital to pond life. Clean it in a bucket of water taken from the pond itself or a rain barrel.

## WHAT YOU WILL NEED

- ✻ Multipurpose compost (if you're starting from scratch)
- ✻ Slow-release fertiliser
- ✻ Water-retaining gel
- ✻ Ericaceous compost (for the gentian)
- ✻ 1 x topiary pyramid box
- ✻ 2 x variegated ivy
- ✻ 2 x winter cherry
- ✻ 2 x gentian
- ✻ 1 x bugle
- ✻ 2 x saxifrage
- ✻ 6 x chrysanthemum

## HOW TO PLANT AN AUTUMN CONTAINER

As the end of August approaches, it's time to consider a fresh new look for some of your containers. If you have some permanent plants in place, such as the box and ivies in this container, then you only need to consider changing the bedding plants.

**1** For a change of season, consider a change of colour for the container. Go over the wooden container with sandpaper and repaint with whatever colour takes your fancy – a sample-size tin of paint is perfect as it contains just enough paint for the job.

**2** Pull out the temporary summer plants. Replace the old compost with some fresh compost that has had slow-release fertiliser and water-retaining gel added to it. Acid-loving gentian will need ericaceous compost.

**3** Plant the temporary autumn plants, filling them in with the fresh compost where needed. Water thoroughly.

**4** To care for your plants, touch the surface of the compost to check whether it needs watering. The cooler weather of autumn means containers shouldn't need watering as often as in summer, but they will still dry out if left too long. Keep an eye out for pests such as aphids, which can quickly multiply in warmer spells. Remove any dead flower heads to keep the display looking tidy.

# YOUR GARDEN IN SEPTEMBER

The approach to autumn can be a magnificent time in the garden and it's when things can get really busy in preparation for cooler weather and spring next year. If you haven't done so already, start tidying your borders, stock up with spring-flowering bulbs, plant shrubs, see to your lawn and keep home-grown crops going strong.

# TOP JOBS THIS MONTH

 ## BORDERS

Tidy annuals and hardy perennials
Dig up hardy annuals
Cut back tall shrubs
Stock up with a wide variety of spring-flowering bulbs
Take cuttings from tender perennials
Plant some shrubs
Make your own compost
Plant autumn and winter containers
Split perennials
Naturalise bulbs

## IN THE GREENHOUSE

Empty the greenhouse and scrub it
Check greenhouse heater
Take cuttings
Prepare hyacinths for Christmas
Give cacti a rest

 ## IN THE FRUIT GARDEN

Harvest apples and pears
Pick autumn raspberries
Prune fruit trees

## ON THE VEG PATCH

Harvest remaining potatoes
Cure squash
Dry off onions
Plant autumn onion sets
Pick sweetcorn and beans
Plant spring greens

 ## LAWNS

Rake, aerate and top dress the lawn
Turf or seed new areas of lawn

 ## PONDS

Net the pond to stop leaves falling in

# Your garden in September

## BORDERS

### Must-do jobs

**Tidy your borders** Summer bedding and hardy perennial plants, such as rudbeckia, coreopsis and asters, will start dying off this month. You'll need to remove any dead growth now to keep your garden tidy and to prevent the build up of diseases. To avoid your plants getting any infections next year, bin or burn any diseased growth. The rest can go on your compost heap. However, you might like to leave the old stems in place until the new year as wildlife will eat seeds and the stems can look very attractive, especially when covered with frost.

**Dig up hardy annuals** Unlike their half-hardy cousins which should still be a blaze of colour at this time of year, most hardy annuals will have run out of steam by now. Collect any seeds you want to keep for next year and store them in labelled envelopes. Dig up the plants and put them in the compost heap. The spare ground can then be planted with bulbs or spring bedding such as wallflowers.

**Cut back tall shrubs** This time of year brings windy weather that can damage plants and even spoil your late-summer display. To reduce the risk, it's worth using canes to prop up top-heavy plants such as dahlias and chrysanthemums. Similarly, quick-growing shrubs like buddleia, lavatera and climbing roses have generally grown quite tall by the end of summer. To stop these being damaged by strong winds, cut back their tallest stems by a third.

## Still time to ...

❋ **... take cuttings** from tender perennials (see page 68). Ensure that you keep your favourite half-hardy plants from one year to the next by taking some cuttings to overwinter indoors.

**Stock up with spring-flowering bulbs** Garden centres and mail-order catalogues will be packed with spring-flowering bulbs. If you're going to buy them, do it now to ensure you get the best specimens and the widest choice of varieties. Look for those that are firm to the touch and don't have any signs of mould. Go for large bulbs as they tend to give the best display. It's best to plant most bulbs as soon as you can, but leave tulip bulbs until November to prevent them becoming diseased.

## Good to get done

### Plant some shrubs

✤ Always start with a decent plant that has lots of healthy new stems and a strong root system.

✤ When positioning your plant, make sure it's not too close to others as they'll compete for moisture and nutrients, which will slow their growth.

✤ Before planting, tease some of the roots away from the original compost. This will help your shrub to quickly root into the soil.

✤ Use your foot to firm the soil in around your new plant so that it's secure and there are no large pockets of air.

✤ Water well then mulch with garden compost or composted bark. Our research shows this technique improves the soil better than digging it in.

**Make your own compost** There's always a lot of clearing and pruning to do in the garden now. That means it's the ideal time to buy or build a new compost bin. Composting conveniently gets rid of your garden waste and produces a handy supply of homemade soil improver.

**Plant containers** Just as your old summer containers are finishing, it's time to plant afresh for autumn and winter colour. There are lots of plants to choose from at the garden centre now. It's worth remembering that plants don't grow much during the colder months, so choose larger ones and plant closely for the best display.

**Divide perennials** As they grow, most perennials gradually spread to form clumps. These clumps become congested, which saps their vigour and reduces flowering. To stop this happening, you should lift, split and replant most perennials roughly every three years. Dig up the

parent plant and split it into chunks, each with its own roots and leaves. These can then be replanted in the ground or pots and any old, worn out pieces can be discarded or put on the compost heap. Now is the ideal time to do this as they're already beginning to die back.

**Naturalise bulbs** Brighten up your lawn for next spring by naturalising some bulbs. Snake's head fritillaries and crocuses work particularly well. For the most natural-looking effect, simply throw the bulbs in the air and plant them where they fall.

**Prune lavender** Give lavender plants a trim to keep them looking neat. If they've grown old and woody, cut them back to a few inches above the bare wood to see if this encourages them to produce new growth lower down.

**Keep patio displays going** The first frosts could still be a month or two away so keep your display of tender plants in pots and hanging baskets looking their best by removing flowers as they fade, watering if the compost feels dry and feeding once a week with a soluble feed. Any slow-release fertiliser used at planting time will now be starting to run out of steam, but feeding plants with a liquid food will perk them up.

## PEST WATCH!

**Vine weevil**
Mid-September is the ideal time to apply a biological control to tackle this annoying pest (see page 88), which eats the roots of plants. By now, any vine weevil eggs laid this summer will have hatched out but won't yet have done much damage. If your watering can's rose keeps blocking when you're applying the control, simply take it off.

**Watch out for wildlife** Many animals are starting to look for winter hiding places so be careful when turning compost heaps and also check bonfires before lighting them.

**Clean paving and decking** Help to reduce the risk of taking a tumble this winter: clean off slippery algae from decking and paving before the rains come. Use a pressure washer or an outdoor cleaner.

# IN THE GREENHOUSE

## Must-do jobs

**Sort out the greenhouse** You're soon going to need your greenhouse to be ready for overwintering tender plants and for sowing seeds in spring. Before you do, it's worth taking time to prepare it.

※ Empty the greenhouse of plants and benches, clear out any rubbish and plant debris. Then give it a good scrub inside and out with hot soapy water, getting into every nook and cranny. This will allow in as much light as possible and will flush out pests and diseases lingering in the corners. If you've got moss growing on windows, an old credit card is great for getting between the glass and frame to get the dirt out.

※ Before putting any plants into your greenhouse, check them over and remove any dead or diseased growth. Also space them as far apart as possible so that there's good airflow around them. Doing both these things helps prevent the build up of diseases in your greenhouse, particularly mildew and soft rot.

※ Finally, check your greenhouse heater to make sure it still works.

**Take cuttings** Rather than overwintering large tender plants such as pelargoniums and fuchsias, take some cuttings now and use these for next year's displays. Once you're sure your cuttings have rooted, you can put any unwieldy parent plants on the compost heap.

## Good to get done

### Prepare hyacinths for Christmas

Prepared hyacinths are specially treated so that they flower in time for Christmas. Plant them now and keep them in a cool, dark, frost-free place, such as a shed or garage. After about eight weeks the flower buds will start to show colour. Once they reach this stage, move your hyacinths to a cool, light spot. Don't move them earlier or the leaves will grow rapidly and cover the flowers. Keep them here for a further two weeks to develop fully, then move them to where you'd like to enjoy their flowering.

**Tend to greenhouse cucumbers and tomatoes** If you haven't already stopped cordon tomato plants, do it now by nipping off the main growing tip. Regularly remove sideshoots and also remove older leaves at the base of the plant to allow air circulation and prevent fungal diseases.

**Give cacti a rest** Don't water or feed cacti and succulents at this time of year, to allow them to have a winter rest. When spring arrives, resume normal care and they'll start growing again.

# IN THE FRUIT GARDEN

## Must-do jobs

**Harvest time** Apples and pears are ready to harvest from September onwards, depending on the variety. You can tell if an apple is ripe by gently lifting the fruit and twisting it. If it's ready, it will come away easily. Any that resist are best left to finish ripening. If you have more fruit than you can use quickly, consider storing the remainder. Pears can be kept in the fridge. Apples will last several months if stored somewhere cool, dark, frost-free and well ventilated – a shed, garage or cellar is ideal for this. You may also want to keep them in plastic bags with small holes in them.

**Pick autumn raspberries** Autumn-fruiting raspberries, such as 'Autumn Bliss', should be at their peak now. You can freeze any you're not able to eat straight away. Wait until late winter before pruning the canes.

## Good to get done

**Prune fruit trees to prevent disease** Fruit tree diseases can worsen over winter so now's a good time to prune out any dead, diseased or sad-looking branches. But don't prune trees that bear fruit containing

stones such as peaches, plums, cherries or apricots, as this can cause disease instead of preventing it. Start by removing any dead, diseased or crossing branches. For most varieties, you can shorten the central shoots by a quarter, then cut sideshoots back to three buds to encourage them to change into fruiting spurs. On varieties that don't produce spurs (tip bearers) – for example, the apple 'Worcester Pearmain' – you only need to cut out some of the shoots that have already borne fruit.

## ON THE VEG PATCH

### Must-do jobs

**Sow outdoors**
- ❊ Winter salads
- ❊ Oriental greens
- ❊ Green manures

**Plant outdoors**
- ❊ Spring cabbage
- ❊ Autumn onion sets

**Harvest**
- ❊ Sweetcorn
- ❊ Potatoes
- ❊ Carrots, beetroots
- ❊ Tomatoes and cucumber
- ❊ Runner, dwarf and climbing beans
- ❊ Last courgettes
- ❊ Onions and shallots
- ❊ Quick crops

## PEST WATCH!

**Insect pests** should become less of a problem as winter approaches, but over-wintering crops, particularly brassicas, will become very attractive to larger pests.

**Pigeons** If you've already covered your crops with fine mesh, leave this in place. If not, bird netting will keep pigeons out, provided it is well supported and clear of the crop. Make sure it is taut and well anchored around the bottom to prevent birds becoming entangled.

**Rabbits** To prevent rabbits enjoying your hard won crops, wire mesh is a good option – bury the bottom to prevent them digging underneath.

### Good to get done

**Harvest remaining potatoes** Maincrop potatoes should have grown to a good size by now so dig them up before the slugs start tunnelling into them. If you can, lift them when the soil is dry as this makes storing them easier and they should then store well for several months. Leave them to dry for a few hours before putting them in boxes or paper sacks. Any that are damaged should be used straight away as they quickly rot in storage.

**Cure squash** Squash should be ripening now. To prepare them for storage to be used over the coming months, it's important to cure the fruits. To do this, cut them with the stalk intact and stand them in a sunny spot. Then move them to a warm room to harden the skins. Finally, put them in a dry, airy place until required.

# 5 MINUTE JOBS

To encourage your **Brussels sprouts** plants to develop properly, cut off the top of the stem. This will encourage the individual sprouts to swell and you can eat the removed top as if it were cabbage.

**Support taller vegetables** like kale with canes in order to prevent them being knocked over by autumn wind.

**167**

**Dry off onions** Lift onions and shallots once their foliage starts to die back. Never bend over the tops as this can cause the bulbs to rot. Leave them in the sun to dry, if possible, but if wet weather is forecast, put them in seed trays and take them into the greenhouse. Store in shallow layers in trays somewhere dry and cool, but frost-free, and they should last well into the spring. Reject any damaged bulbs or ones that have bolted and use these first. Undamaged bulbs can be stored in nets or plaited into strings and hung.

**Plant autumn onion sets** The variety 'Troy' will store for ages, so you could plant lots of these onions and not bother with spring sets. 'Senshyu Yellow' is also useful as an early crop before 'Troy' is ready.

## Still time to ...

❀ **... sow green manure** (see page 151). Fill any patches of ground that you don't intend to use for winter crops to improve the fertility and structure of the soil.

**Pick sweetcorn** Sweetcorn should be ready from mid-August onwards. Pick the cobs when the tassels on top have turned brown and shrivelled. Check by peeling back the sheath and press a fingernail into a grain. If clear liquid spurts out, leave them a little longer until it's milky.

**Runner and climbing beans** should keep going, as long as you pick them regularly and water them frequently in dry spells. A good soak once a week is best. Later sowings of dwarf beans should also crop for a while yet.

**Winter salads** It's now too late to keep sowing quick summer crops, but there are several winter-hardy salads worth trying, such a mizuna, claytonia, mustards, endive and pak choi. If you want to sow direct, prepare a seedbed (see pages 60–1) and give it a thorough soaking a day before. Use slug pellets or other controls to prevent the seedlings being eaten. An alternative is to start them off in module trays to plant out after four weeks or so. As the weather cools, cover them with a couple of layers of fleece and they should last until spring.

**Spring greens** Plant out spring greens sown last month or bought as plants. If the ground is dry, give it a thorough soaking the day before. Space the plants 15cm apart with 30cm between rows. This allows for alternate plants to be harvested as leafy spring greens; the remainder will heart up later in the spring. Net the plants to prevent pigeons from eating them.

## LAWNS

### Must-do jobs

**Winter health** September is a key month for getting your lawn into shape. These steps will help your grass stay greener and more wear-resistant.

**Rake** Grass clippings and moss accumulate in the lower layers of the lawn to form a dense material called thatch. It's best to rake ('scarify') this out so that water and nutrients can reach the grass roots beneath. A spring-tine rake is ideal for the job. If you have a large lawn, you might want to hire a scarifier for about £40 a day.

**Aerate** The soil beneath your turf can become compacted and drain poorly, which encourages moss and lawn diseases. Remedy this by aerating the turf using a fork to stab and lift the turf slightly. Do this all over your lawn. Alternatively, if you've got a large lawn, you can hire an aerator machine for about £12 a day, which removes cores of earth.

**Thicken turf** Lightly fork bald areas of lawn and sprinkle on some grass seed. It grows quickly at this time of year and will plug the gaps before winter. Also repair the frayed edges of your lawn by cutting out the damaged section with a spade and turning it around. Use grass seed to fill any holes left.

**Top dress** Brush in a top dressing to keep it aerated and help to level the surface. You can either buy ready-made top dressing or make your own with six parts sharp sand, three parts sieved soil and one part sieved garden compost. Apply 1kg of dressing per m$^2$ and then brush it into the ground.

**Feed** Autumn lawn feed doesn't give much long-term benefit, so for the best results, use lawn sand instead. This helps to green up the grass and control moss – it is also much cheaper than lawn feed.

## PONDS

### Must-do jobs

**Stop leaves falling in** Rotting leaves are one of the main causes of murky water in ponds. Stop them getting in by netting ponds and cutting off dying leaves from pond plants before they fall into the water.

## WHAT YOU WILL NEED

- Spade
- Rake
- General-purpose fertiliser
- Garden canes
- Turf or grass seed
- Plank
- Sharp knife

## HOW TO LAY TURF AND SOW GRASS SEED

Whether you're starting a new lawn from scratch or adding to an existing one, you face the same dilemma: should you opt for the quick fix of turf or take your time and grow it from seed? Whichever you go for, follow this step-by-step advice.

### Ground preparation

The initial ground preparation is the same whether you are using seed or turf – it's worth the effort to get a good finish.

**1** Dig the area roughly to loosen it and remove any existing plants, especially any tough perennial weeds such as dandelions. Rake the area to create a fine surface, and remove any larger stones, roots or other debris as you go.

**2** Tread it thoroughly, shuffling backwards and putting the weight on your heels to firm the soil and eliminate any soft spots. Rake over again to level the surface and repeat the process.

**3** Add a scattering of general-purpose fertiliser – about 35g per m² of Growmore is ideal. Use canes spaced at 1m intervals (see Sowing grass seed, opposite) to achieve an even spread.

### Laying turf

**1** Lay the first roll along one edge of the new lawn. Stand on a plank to spread your weight and lay the next roll up to it, staggering the ends. Butt adjacent rolls tightly. Fill any larger gaps with loose soil.

**2** Use a sharp knife to cut round hard edges. The lawn surface should be slightly proud of paths or edging strips so you can run the mower over the edge.

**3** Cut neat edges against your borders using a half-moon edging knife. Use the side of a plank to help you cut straight edges or a length of hose to cut curves.

## HOW TO CHOOSE TURF

Unroll some turves and check the quality. Turves should be of even thickness between 13 and 18mm thick. The grass should be dense and mid- to dark green with no yellow or brown patches. The turves should hold together when lifted carefully and the underside should be moist. Reject any poor-quality turf that is dry or shrivelled, looks diseased or contains weeds.

### Sowing grass seed

**1** Lay garden canes across the area at 1m intervals to help sow the correct rate of grass seed.

**2** Weigh out 35g of seed and tip it into a plastic cup. Draw a line on the cup and use this cup to judge the amount for each 1m square. Try to scatter it as evenly as possible – scatter half in one direction and half in the other.

**3** Remove the canes and rake the area gently to work the seed into the soil. Water the area in dry weather and protect the seed from birds by using netting or bird scarers until a green fuzz appears.

# YOUR GARDEN IN OCTOBER

Never let it be said that autumn and early winter is a time of rest for a gardener. This month should see you collecting leaves, planting a tree or two as well as some climbers, protecting plants from frost and storing apples for the months ahead.

# TOP JOBS THIS MONTH

## BORDERS

Bring plants indoors
Protect tender plants
Clear paths of leaves
Make your own leaf mould
Make a leaf bin
Give wildlife a helping hand
Raise containers
Buy and plant bedding
Plant bulbs
Plant a tree or climber
Start mulching
Top up paths with bark

## IN THE GREENHOUSE

Remove shading from the windows
Insulate the greenhouse
Force some bulbs
Plant overwintering crops

## IN THE FRUIT GARDEN

Store apples

## ON THE VEG PATCH

Sow salads and oriental greens
Improve the soil
Harvest chard and leaf beet
Eat autumn cabbages and cauliflowers
Dig up root crops
Plant onion sets and garlic
Harvest pumpkins and winter squash

## LAWNS

Rake, aerate and top dress the lawn
Turf or seed new areas of lawn

## PONDS

Net the pond
Remove dead growth

## BORDERS

### Must-do jobs

**Bring plants indoors**
Frosts are very likely this month so it's a good idea to bring in your tender perennials to stop them being damaged or killed. Evergreen plants, such as pelargoniums, will carry on growing so they'll need to go somewhere bright and frost-free, such as a greenhouse or conservatory. Plants that lose their leaves or die back completely, like fuchsias and cannas, can be kept in the dark – a frost-free shed or garage is ideal. To save room, you could take some late cuttings and dispose of the parent plant.

### Still time to ...

❋ ... **cut back perennials** (see page 159).

❋ ... **give your conifer hedges a final cut** if they're looking shaggy (see page 131).

❋ ... **divide perennials** (see page 161).

**Protect tender plants** It's not always possible to bring in large tender plants like palms so you'll need to frost-proof them. Insert canes all around the plant to support a snug jacket of garden fleece and anchor fleece at the base with soil. For gunnera, cut down the giant leaves and protect the tender crowns of the plant with straw. Place the old leaves on top to prevent the straw blowing away. For particularly tender plants, pack straw inside the fleece. Don't forget to check the covering is still in place after windy weather.

**Clear paths of leaves** It's important to clear up fallen leaves in the garden for a number of reasons – the main one is because they can make paths and patios very slippery and dangerous to walk on. Where the leaves fall on your lawn, they block out the light and, as a result, can cause the grass to die off if covered for too long. There is no need for you to tidy up leaves on borders, however, because they act as a mulch and also as shelter for overwintering creatures.

**Make your own leaf mould**
Collecting fallen leaves gives you the opportunity to make this great soil improver. Simply bag up the leaves into a black polythene sack, make a few holes in it for air, and wait around 18 months for them to break down. A quick and easy way to clear the lawn is to run over the leaves with the lawnmower. It not only picks up the leaves, but also chops them up – and shredded leaves rot down in 12 months (see overleaf for a guide to making a leaf bin).

**Make a leaf bin** An alternative to bagging leaves is to make a leaf bin. It provides the perfect place to leave them so they rot down into leaf mould.

❋ Hammer four wooden fencing stakes into the ground in a square shape.

❋ Wrap chicken wire all the way around the frame and fix it in place with some wire.

❋ Fill the bin. Use deciduous leaves, as evergreens take longer to rot and a good leaf mould should be ready after 18 months.

**Give wildlife a helping hand** Give wildlife somewhere to hide during the cold months by heaping up some leaves in a quiet corner or making a pile of old logs. If you build a bonfire, surround it with a wire fence to stop creatures getting inside and when lighting it, do so on one side to create an escape route for any animals that may have found their way in.

# 5 MINUTE JOB

**Raise containers** Wet compost can kill winter container displays, so improve the drainage of your pots by raising them off the ground. You can buy decorative 'pot feet' or just use a piece of wood or a brick.

## Good to get done

**Prepare to feed the birds** Birds are prone to several nasty diseases that can build up on dirty bird tables and feeders, so clean them regularly using hot, soapy water and a stiff brush. Be sure to remove any food residues and droppings. Wash once a fortnight. Put the feeders in the same place every time you fill them so the birds learn where to come and make sure the feeders never go empty.

**Plant bulbs** Plan ahead for colour next year by planting bulbs now. October is the ideal month to plant summer-flowering lilies and there's still time to get your spring blooms too. Hold fire with tulips until November. You may find some bargains available as garden centres aim to create space for their Christmas displays.

**Buy and plant bedding** Plan ahead for colour during the winter and into the spring with a trip to the garden centre to buy bedding plants such as wallflowers, violas, sweet Williams and forget-me-nots. It pays to be early to get the best selection of varieties and colours. Bare-root wallflowers are a traditional choice for spring colour. Make sure the plants are not floppy and put them in as soon as you get them home.

# ✤ Your garden in October

### Plant a tree or climber

Autumn is a good time for putting in new plants, as the soil is still warm after summer and, with plenty of rain usually forecast for the UK, plants should establish quickly without needing much additional watering from you. When planting a tree, check that you plant it at the same depth that it was in the pot. It will also need staking to anchor it and stop it moving around while the new roots are forming. Attach the tree to the stake with a tree tie and check it every few months to make sure it still fits well. Finally, add some mulch around the tree for a nutritious start.

❉ To give your climber something to scale, we recommend using horizontal wires, spaced 30cm apart, which you can fix to your walls and fences. Leave a 5cm gap between the wires and the wall/fence.

❉ The soil at the base of a wall or fence can be very dry, so plant the climber 30cm away from it. Before planting, tease out the plant's roots a little from the original compost as this will help it establish.

❉ Plant the climber at an angle, leaning towards the wall or fence. Remove the cane supporting the climber and train its stems along the wires using soft string.

❉ Finally, water your plant well and mulch with garden compost or composted bark. Keep it well-watered while it establishes.

**Start mulching** Autumn and spring are good times to cover bare ground with a mulch, such as garden compost, to trap the moisture in the soil. Be sure to remove any weeds before you begin and the mulch should help prevent new ones appearing. Mulches based on organic matter will also gradually rot down and improve the soil. Make sure you put it on in a layer about 5cm deep.

**Toadstools** Don't be surprised to see toadstools popping up around the garden at this time of year. Most are no cause for concern as they don't actively harm plants. However, a few – such as honey fungus on woody plants and fairy rings in the lawn – are a problem. There is no chemical control for either fungus. The best advice for honey fungus is to dig up and destroy the affected plant. For fairy rings, spike, water and feed any dead areas of grass that they cause. Digging out the rings is a huge amount of work and removing the toadstools won't reduce the risk of infection to any great extent.

**Top up paths with bark** With the garden starting to clear, it's a good time to do maintenance jobs such as topping up paths with fresh bark chips.

**Carry on deadheading** While most plants have run out of steam by now, some super-performers, such as these alstroemerias, are still blooming their socks off. To keep them going for as long as possible, keep removing the dead flowers as soon as they fade.

## IN THE GREENHOUSE

### Must-do jobs

**Get ready for winter** With falling light levels, it's a good idea to remove shading. Netting can be stored for next year, while shading paint can be wiped off.

**Insulate the greenhouse** Prepare for the coming cold weather by insulating your greenhouse. Bubble plastic can be bought off the roll at garden centres. It can be attached to wooden-framed greenhouses using drawing pins. For attaching bubble wrap to metal frames, buy the special fixings that are available in garden centres.

**Sow sweet peas** For the earliest flowers next year, it's worth sowing some sweet peas in pots now to plant out after the first frosts (see pages 60–1). Their roots are very long so it's best to use a deep container. Rootrainers are good as their deep modules can be opened up to minimise disturbance at planting time. Soaking seeds or chipping their coats before sowing is unnecessary. They'll need to stay in a coldframe or cold greenhouse over winter and need wrapping up on frosty nights, but you'll be rewarded with scented blooms from June onwards.

## Good to get done
### Force some bulbs

It's common to grow prepared hyacinths at this time of year so that they flower in time for Christmas (see page 164), but you can use the same technique to bring other bulbs into early flower indoors – although not quite in time for the festivities. Try these bulbs:

* *Crocus* 'Snow Bunting'
* *Lachenalia aloides* var. *quadricolor*
* *Muscari botryoides* 'Album'
* *Narcissus* 'Sir Winston Churchill'
* *Narcissus* 'Tête-à-tête'
* *Scilla mischtschenkoana*
* *Tulipa* 'Peach Blossom'

**Plant overwintering crops** If you have empty space in the greenhouse borders or in containers, it's worth trying to overwinter salads, carrots and oriental greens under cover.

## IN THE FRUIT GARDEN

### Must-do jobs

**Store apples** Pest- and disease-free fruit can be stored in a cool, dark place for later use. Damaged fruit can either be eaten immediately or you can make them into pies or purées for freezing.

## DISEASE WATCH!

**Grey mould** Keep an eye on brassicas such as kale and Brussels sprouts, removing any yellowing leaves you find and dispose of them, but not in your compost bin. This will help prevent problems with grey mould.

## ON THE VEG PATCH

### Must-do jobs

#### Sow outdoors
✿ Winter salads and oriental greens

#### Plant outdoors
✿ Autumn onion sets
✿ Garlic in the south

#### Harvest
✿ Autumn cabbage and cauliflower
✿ Maincrop beetroot, carrot, parsnip, turnip
✿ Leeks
✿ Chard and leaf beet
✿ Last runner beans
✿ Pumpkins and winter squash
✿ First kale, Brussels sprouts and sprouting broccoli

### Improve the soil

Unless you're planning to fill your whole vegetable plot with winter crops, some of it will be empty until spring. If so, it's a chance to improve the soil. If your soil is heavy clay, dig it now and leave it untended. Hard frost will break down the lumps of clay, giving you a finer surface to work on next year. Alternatively, you can sow mustard or phacelia as green manures (see page 151).

## Good to get done

**Plant autumn and winter salads** It's a bit late to sow winter salads direct into the ground, although you could try some of the hardiest types such as mizuna or rocket. Those started in pots or modular trays can be planted out now and should stand more chance of avoiding the local slug and snail population. If frost is likely, put fleece over the salads.

**Harvest chard and leaf beet** These crops come into their own now. Both are hardy enough to survive through the winter and produce a useful flush of new growth in spring, before they bolt.

**Eat autumn cabbages and cauliflowers** Cut cauliflowers as soon as the heads reach a good size and the tiny flower buds are still tight. Autumn cabbages are best used before the first severe frosts, but winter cabbages such as 'January King' and savoys can be left until needed.

**Harvest kales** Varieties such as 'Cavalo Nero' and 'Scarlet Curled' are hardy and you can pick leaves through the winter.

**Dig up root crops** Beetroot, carrots, parsnips and leeks should be ready to dig now as required. They keep well in the ground, though in cold areas cover the rows with straw or fleece to protect them from frost.

**Brussels sprouts and sprouting broccoli** will start to crop from now until early spring, depending on the variety.

**Plant onion sets** If you haven't already done so, plant autumn onion sets when the soil is still warm and moist. If the soil is hard, it's worth preparing a loose seedbed to avoid damaging the sets; plant them with a dibber or trowel.

**Plant garlic** Garlic is available for autumn planting and this gives it a head start for next year. The plant needs a cold period to produce good bulbs, so it can be planted until February. If you order now, there will be a better choice of variety.

**Harvest pumpkins and winter squash** These should be ripening off nicely now and the foliage will be dying down – the first autumn frost will finish it off. If the weather is cool and wet, move the fruits into the greenhouse or a sunny windowsill to finish ripening so that they store well. Pumpkins won't keep much beyond Halloween, so use these first. Winter squash should keep until early spring at least. Cure them by keeping them in a warm room for two weeks, then somewhere dry and cool but frost-free.

# 5 MINUTE JOBS

**Prune asparagus** Asparagus ferns turn yellow as they die down. Cut them off at ground level to make space for next year's crop. Remove any weeds at the same time as asparagus hates competition.

**Check nets** regularly and keep them clear of plants to keep pigeons off your winter brassicas, such as Brussels sprouts.

## LAWNS

### Must-do jobs

**Carry on the good work** If you didn't get the chance to care for your lawn in September (see page 171), it is still not too late to get out there and do it early in October.

## PONDS

### Must-do jobs

**Remove dead growth** As aquatic plants die back in autumn anyway, it's worth also cutting them back now, before any of their dead growth falls into the water. Decaying growth can taint the water, reducing light available to other aquatic life such as fish and frogs, and can encourage algae to grow next year.

### Still time to ...

✿ **... net the pond**. Fish out any leaves that have fallen in and then cover the pond with netting to stop more getting in.

## WHAT YOU WILL NEED

* Wooden crate
* Nails
* Translucent plastic envelope stiffener (often known as 'flyweight') available from newsagents, or Perspex
* Garden twine
* Hammer
* Hand saw

## HOW TO MAKE A COLDFRAME

This attractive coldframe is ideal for propagating or for hardening off young plants before planting out. You might be able to find a crate such as this from a pick-your-own fruit grower and if you are hoping for a completely recycled project, look for old, rusty nails, too. Although removing the sides of the crate was a fiddly job, the whole coldframe only takes about 30 minutes to make.

**1** Tap and lever off the upper sides of the crate using a claw hammer and screwdriver. Take care not to damage the slats too much as they will be needed again later. If possible, save the old nails as well!

**2** Cut the old side slats in half diagonally so that when they're nailed back on, the frame has sloping sides. Cut the front slat to fit in with the adapted side slats, but leave the rear slat intact.

**3** Nail the sawn slats back onto the crate so that they rest tightly above the lower slats without a gap. We used the original rusty nails but if yours are too bent or rusty, use new galvanised nails.

**4** Using a fine-toothed hand saw for the neatest possible job, saw off the upright corner pieces in line with the newly adjusted slats. If necessary, sand down any rough or snagged edges.

**5** Hammer a small nail into the centre of the upper slat at the front. Place an offcut from the uprights behind the nail, inside the crate and hammer it in so it's just protruding on the outside.

**6** Similarly, from the outside hammer a nail into both back corners. Again, allow the nails to protrude a little so that string can be attached to them. Cut a piece of flyweight or Perspex to form a lid.

**7** Tie a piece of garden string to a nail at the back and bring it diagonally across the lid, hooking it under the front nail. Attach the string to the other back nail by making a loop and hooking it over. Put your plants in the frame and enjoy the results.

# YOUR GARDEN IN NOVEMBER

Remember, there's still plenty to do in November! Now's the time to get your borders looking shipshape as well as giving vines a prune. You can also get those tulips in the ground and sow broad beans and hardy peas. To finish everything off, why not bring some fragrant viburnum inside for a scented lift, too?

# TOP JOBS THIS MONTH

## BORDERS
Plant tulips
Order seeds and plants
Catch weeds
Plant perennials
Buy bare-root plants
Gather fallen leaves
Continue to plant bedding
Care for chrysanthemums
Protect valuable pots by using bubble wrap
Remove stakes and supports
Check bonfire sites for hedgehogs

## IN THE GREENHOUSE
Prevent disease by picking over plants regularly
Buy hippeastrum
Bring forced bulbs indoors to enjoy

## IN THE FRUIT GARDEN
Put grease bands around fruit trees
Prune vines

## ON THE VEG PATCH
Sow hardy peas and broad beans
Harvest winter crops
Tidy up summer crops
Put away garden fleece
Tend to your compost
Cover brassicas with netting

## LAWNS
Give your mower some TLC
Cut grass with blades on high

## PONDS
Prevent water from freezing by floating a ball on the surface

## BORDERS

### Must-do jobs

**Plant tulips** November is the traditional time to plant tulips as there is a reduced risk of them getting the fungal disease, tulip fire (the fungus can cause plants to rot and not develop properly – shoots can emerge malformed). Plant them 10–20cm apart and at three times or more of their own depth of soil as shallow planting is a common cause for them failing to flower for a second year. If squirrels are a problem, cover the soil surface with chicken wire to stop them digging up the bulbs.

**Order seeds and plants** Catalogues are full of tempting new varieties of flowers and veg. It's worth ordering early to guarantee the varieties you want, especially for seed potatoes and plug plants, which tend to sell out quickest.

**Catch weeds** Like most plants, weeds shouldn't be putting on much growth during the colder weather. This makes it a good time to go round and catch as many as you can before they burst into life when things warm up again. Perennial weeds such as creeping buttercup (pictured right) should always be dug up or they'll resprout.

## Good to get done

**Bring the beauty indoors** If the weather has taken a turn for the worse and you don't fancy loitering outdoors for too long, bring the beauty of the garden indoors. There are several plants that come into their own during winter, from fragrant shrubs such as viburnums to tiny flowers such as violas. Bringing them indoors is often the best way of appreciating their beautiful scents.

**Plant perennials** While your summer borders are still fresh in your mind, it's a good time to fill any gaps with new plants, such as this hardy geranium, and move any plants that you felt didn't work in their current spot. While the soil is generally moist at this time of year, don't forget to water them if the weather turns dry in the couple of months following planting as their roots will still be establishing.

## Still time to...

❋ ... **gather fallen leaves**. Put them in black polythene sacks to make leaf mould (see pages 179–80).

❋ ... **plant bedding**. Wallflowers, forget-me-nots and bellis are just some of the bedding plants that can be planted now for colour in the coming months (see page 182).

**Buy bare-root plants** The cheapest way of buying many woody plants, such as shrubs, fruit, hedging and roses, is to get them as 'bare-root' plants without a pot and compost. Garden centres and mail-order companies both stock them. If postal deliveries arrive before you're ready to plant them, put them in a bucket of water for a few hours and then roughly plant them in a quiet spot until you're ready to move them to their final position.

**Deadhead patio plants** Keep your displays looking fresh and encourage plants to keep flowering by removing blooms as they fade. It will also help to stop fungal diseases attacking the dying flowers. Don't over-water your displays at this time of year – the plants aren't in full growth so don't require much water.

**Cut back dahlias** Once the frost has blackened the leaves of dahlias, cut back the plants to ground level. In well drained soils, dahlias can simply be left in the ground and covered with a 10–15cm deep layer of compost or bark to protect them from frosts. For colder areas and heavier soils, lift the plants, store them indoors over winter and replant them outdoors the following spring.

**Care for chrysanthemums** After years in the fashion doldrums, chrysanths are shining again. They provide glorious colour when most other plants have given up the ghost. It's best to grow most of them in pots so they can be moved to the protection of the greenhouse when the weather takes a turn for the worse. Once flowering is over, the plants can be dried off, cut back and stored in a frost-free place, ready to replant in spring.

**Protect valuable pots with bubble wrap** Winter frosts can sometimes penetrate pots and expand the water inside, so stop treasured pots shattering as a result of this by covering them with a layer of bubble wrap.

**Prevent rabbit damage with a tree guard** Stop hungry rabbits attacking your trees by placing a tree guard around the trunk.

# 5 MINUTE JOBS

**Remove any stakes** and supports that are left in the ground after you've cut back plants, and put them away for the winter.

**Check bonfire sites** for hedgehogs before lighting, and only light one side so that animals have a chance to escape.

# ✿ Your garden in November

## IN THE GREENHOUSE

### Must-do jobs
**Prevent disease**
A therapeutic job for both you and your plants is to pick over them once a week and remove any dead leaves or flowers that you find. It's the sort of task that can be very relaxing after a busy day. By removing the dead material promptly, you'll be stopping fungal diseases in their tracks as these are the number one killer of greenhouse plants during the damp winter months. It's also worth sweeping the floor to collect up any material that's fallen off the plants.

### Good to get done
**Buy hippeastrum**
Buy hippeastrum (amaryllis) now to get the best selection of bulbs, but hold off planting until February. Bulbs planted immediately tend to struggle in the low light levels of winter. By planting later on, the emergence of the leaves will coincide with the natural increase in day length.

**Enjoy flowers indoors** Look out for forced bulbs, such as paper-white narcissus, at the garden centre. It's a lot easier to buy them ready to flower than forcing them at home. Pot them up into decorative containers and enjoy them indoors in a cool, well-lit spot. Narcissus grow quite tall, so add some peasticks or canes to support them.

### Still time to ...

✿ **... insulate the greenhouse.** Trap heat by covering the glass with bubble plastic, which is available off the roll at garden centres.

# IN THE FRUIT GARDEN

## Must-do jobs

**Put grease bands around fruit trees** Trap winter moths by placing grease bands around the trunk and stake of fruit trees. They should be placed about 45cm above soil level and left in place until April. For older trees with rough bark, use paint-on grease. This will prevent the wingless female moths crawling up the tree to lay their eggs. Moth eggs hatch in spring and the caterpillars attack the leaves.

**Prune vines** Be sure to prune grapes before Christmas or they'll bleed from their pruning wounds.

❋ For plants trained using the guyot system, remove the horizontal arm that fruited in summer. Tie down one or two vertical shoots to the lowest wires and cut them back to 60–90cm. Cut the remaining central shoot back to two or three buds.

❋ For plants trained using the rod and spur system, cut back the side branches to one or two buds from the main stem.

## Good to get done

**Prune blackcurrants** For the biggest crops, you need to prune blackcurrants every year. As most fruit forms on stems produced the previous season, encourage new growth by removing about a quarter of the older stems. These are either grey or black in colour. Remove them at the base. Use loppers for the job as the shoots are too thick for secateurs. If you have a plant that hasn't been pruned for a few years, cut out more of the older wood. Alternatively, cut the whole plant back to ground level next winter.

**Divide rhubarb** Larger rhubarb plants can be lifted and divided in the same way as ornamental perennials (see page 206). Chop the plant into sections with a fork or spade, ensuring that each one has a bud. The buds should be just above the soil surface when you replant them.

## Still time to ...

✿ **... plant winter salads**. Look forward to fresh salad leaves, such as this purple pak choi, in the colder months by planting now. Cover them with fleece to keep off the worst of the weather and pests such as pigeons.

## ON THE VEG PATCH

### Must-do jobs
**Sow outdoors**
✿ Over-winter peas and broad beans
✿ Winter salads under cover

**Harvest**
✿ Carrots, parsnips, leeks
✿ Beetroot
✿ Brussels sprouts and sprouting broccoli
✿ Winter cabbage and cauliflower
✿ Winter salads

**Tidy up** Remove the remains of summer crops and add them to the compost heap. Put away garden fleece and fine mesh that's not in use to be reused next year. Bring canes indoors as they last longer with a bit of TLC.

**Tend to your compost** Ideally if you operate a twin-bin system, the contents of one bin should be ready to use now. Remove this and store it under cover for use in the spring. The compost can also be used as a mulch on raised beds, if you use a no-dig regime, but bear in mind that soluble nutrients will be washed out by the winter rain. You can now transfer the contents of the second bin, mixing it as you go, to complete the composting process. Place a square of old carpet or similar on top to insulate it and make sure that the bin is covered to prevent it from getting too wet over winter.

### Good to get done

**Dig up Jerusalem artichokes** You'll be surprised by how many Jerusalem artichoke tubers will be hiding in the soil when you come to dig them up. Very knobbly tubers are a pain to peel so you might want to avoid the hassle and compost them. If you don't want to grow Jerusalem artichokes in the same spot, you'll have to be very thorough, removing any tubers you find or you'll have a forest of plants next summer.

**PEST WATCH!**

**Pigeons** Cover brassicas such as kale with netting to stop pigeons shredding the leaves. Use 15cm plastic pea and bean mesh, and extend it 60cm beyond the outer rows. Hold tightly in place with canes.

**Harvest leeks** Dig up leeks as and when you need them as they're fine to stay in the ground until you're ready. When preparing them in the kitchen, cut them down the middle and fan out under a running tap to wash out any soil that's caught inside.

**Sow broad beans** November is the traditional time to sow broad beans. Choose a hardy variety such as 'Aquadulce Claudia' and it should crop a couple of weeks ahead of a spring sowing. Choose a sheltered spot with well-drained soil if possible and sow in double rows or blocks with 20cm between plants each way. Much depends on where you are and the kind of winter you get, so keep some seeds back for sowing in spring.

**Sow hardy peas** The same applies to hardy peas – varieties such as 'Feltham First' and 'Douce Provence', and the mangetout 'Oregon Sugar Pod'. These will produce a valuable early crop and will be free of pea moth. In a very cold or exposed area a sowing of peas in a vacant greenhouse border might be a better bet. They should be out of the way by the time space is needed for the tomatoes.

**Protect your crops from mice** Wherever you sow over-wintering peas and beans, you'll need to protect them from mice, which excavate the seeds, and slugs and snails, which graze on the shoots. Take precautions against both (see page 40).

# 5 MINUTE JOB

**Look after Brussels sprouts** These plants can get a bit large and unwieldy by this time of year. To avoid picking your sprouts off the ground when you come to harvest, stake plants now with sturdy canes. Every week or so, remove any dead or dying leaves around the bottom of plants. This helps remove a source of disease, allows air to circulate and makes picking the sprouts easier. They develop from the bottom up, so pick in this order.

# LAWNS

## Must-do jobs

**Give your mower some TLC** The cooler weather sees grass slowing down in growth, although you may need to trim it during any milder spells before the main season begins again in spring. Now is a good time to give the mower some attention.

🌸 Give grass a final cut with blades on the highest setting to tidy up its appearance. It's also a neat way of collecting any leaves that have fallen on the lawn.

🌸 Clean away any grass stuck to the bottom of the mower. An old plant label or piece of wood makes a useful tool for this job.

🌸 Check to see whether the blades are blunt. Use a sharpening stone to put a good edge on metal blades or, alternatively, buy a replacement blade.

# PONDS

## Must-do jobs

**Avoid freezing** Put a floating ball or piece of polystyrene in ponds to stop the water freezing. Avoid ice forming as it traps methane gas released by decaying vegetation, which can be deadly to fish. Concrete pools are also vulnerable to cracking as the ice expands.

## HOW TO DIVIDE PLANTS

Create new perennials using this easy method of division, which reinvigorates old plants.

### What is it?

Many perennial plants grow in an ever-widening clump. After two to three years they begin to die out in the centre and look more like a ring than a clump. To keep the plants vigorous and blooming, you can divide them. Dividing perennial plants gives you healthier, longer-living plants and the bonus of more plants.

### When to do it?

November through to March (dormant season), although some – primulas and bearded irises – are best done after flowering.

### How to divide potted plants

**1** Use clump-forming perennials with healthy shoots. Remove the plant from the pot and then – using a clean, sharp knife – cut the root ball in half.

**2** Once the original clump is cut in half, split further into manageable sections. Each of these should contain both shoots and roots.

**3** Pot up small clumps into suitable containers. Plant out in the garden after two to three months.

## How to divide plants in the ground

**1** Select a healthy, clump-forming plant. Dig it up using a fork.

**2** Insert two forks back-to-back with their tines interlocking. Split the clump in two by pushing the fork handles together. Continue splitting and dividing until you have several pieces, each with its own roots and shoots.

**3** Replant the pieces into well-prepared ground.

### Some plants the technique is suitable for

* Delphiniums
* Hostas
* Asters
* Herbaceous campanulas
* Hardy geraniums
* Shasta daisies
* Yarrow and grasses
* Flag irises
* Lily of the valley

# YOUR GARDEN IN DECEMBER

The Christmas spirit is in the air, but so are the frosts, so make sure you protect your tender plants. You can give your garden some colour with dogwood and cyclamen now, and gather holly and ivy to brighten up your home and create some festive cheer.

# TOP JOBS THIS MONTH

 **BORDERS**

Choose a Christmas tree
Prune birch and acers
Gather decorations for indoors
Add some extra colour to the garden
Look out for bulb bargains
Beward pansy sickness
Take hardwood cuttings
Plant winter stems
Take root cuttings
Tie in wall shrubs
Check tree stakes and ties
Pick up diseased leaves

 **IN THE GREENHOUSE**

Buy a poinsettia or two
Keep your Christmas hyacinths cool
Check that the greenhouse heater
is still working

 **IN THE FRUIT GARDEN**

Remove mummified fruit from your
apple trees
Plant new fruit trees and bushes
Plant bare-root fruit

 **ON THE VEG PATCH**

Sow hardy peas and broad beans
Get digging
Check stored vegetables
Harvest winter crops, such as
brassicas, beetroot and root veg

 **LAWNS**

Re-cut all your lawn edges for an
instant lift

 **PONDS**

Prevent water from freezing by
floating a ball on the surface

## BORDERS

### Must-do jobs
**Choose a Christmas tree** If you buy a cut tree, both Norway Spruce and Nordmann Fir will last about three weeks with a good supply of water. If you've bought a cut tree, as soon as you get it home, place it in a bucket of water until you want to bring it indoors. Saw 3cm off the cut end and use a stand or bucket that holds water. It may not have roots, but a tree like this will drink more than half a litre (a pint) a day, so always keep it topped up. Container-grown trees also last well and can be subsequently planted in the garden after Christmas. Potted trees that have been dug up from the ground don't do so well.

### Good to get done
**Prune birch and acers** Do any pruning needed on acers and birch before the end of the year when they're dormant to stop the wounds bleeding sap and weakening the plant. The main job is to remove any dead or diseased growth, cutting back to a healthy bud.

### Still time to ...

✿ **... take hardwood cuttings**. Many shrubs, including rubus, dogwood (cornus), buddleja and willow (salix) can be propagated from autumn to spring by taking hardwood cuttings (see pages 34–5).

**Gather decorations** With Christmas just around the corner, now's the time to gather natural decorations such as holly and ivy. If you want your holly to have berries, cover it with netting to protect it from birds until you're ready to cut it.

**Add some extra colour** Hardy *Cyclamen coum* will bloom through the winter months, producing a carpet of pink or white blooms set off against silvery, dark green leaves. It's best to buy them when they're already in growth as you can select the plants with the strongest leaf markings – this varies quite considerably as plants are raised from seed. Plant them in a partially shaded spot, such as under trees or shrubs, in well-drained soil.

**Look out for bulb bargains** It's late in the season for planting bulbs so there are bargains to be had as garden centres heavily discount their remaining stock. The following bulbs can be planted as late as December and still have a good show the following spring: *Tulipa* 'Queen of the Night', *Allium* 'Purple Sensation', *Fritillaria* 'Maxima Lutea' and April-flowering daffodils. Of course, this also applies to any bulbs you may have bought earlier in the season but have forgotten to plant until now, so have a quick trawl of the shed to see if you can find any overlooked bags. When selecting which to buy, check that bulbs are firm to the touch and that there are no signs of mould.

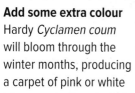

## DISEASE WATCH!

**Pansy sickness** This is a fungal disease that causes the whole plant to turn yellow and die off. There's nothing you can treat the plants with so the best advice is to remove them and throw them away. The disease is carried in the soil so don't grow pansies and violas in the same spot year after year.

### Plant winter stems

If your garden is looking a little dull now the autumn colour has faded, why not add some plants with colourful winter stems? Dogwoods, willow and rubus all offer brightly coloured stems that are revealed once their leaves have fallen. The youngest stems produce the brightest colours, so to encourage your plants to produce lots of these, cut back all of the stems to two or three buds from the base every year in early spring. For shrub planting instructions, see page 160.

### Tidy perennials

Cut back any perennials that have started to look untidy and put them on the compost heap.

### Tie in wall shrubs

Check that all growth is tied in to the wall or fence to protect it from wind damage and to keep it looking tidy.

## 5 MINUTE JOBS

**Check tree stakes and ties** to see if they need loosening, replacing or removing.

**Pick up diseased leaves** – good garden hygiene helps prevent diseases spreading year on year.

# IN THE GREENHOUSE

## Must-do jobs

**Buy a poinsettia or two** For many people, Christmas wouldn't be the same without the cheery red bracts of poinsettia. When buying one, avoid plants stored outside as they like the warmth. At home, position them in a well-lit spot, away from draughts. Don't forget there is now a range of different colours available to enjoy.

**Keep your Christmas hyacinths cool** The bulbs that you planted in September (see page 164) will start to show colour, so move them to a cool place. In a warm spot, leaves will grow rapidly and obscure the flowers. The bulbs can be planted in the garden after flowering but may take a year or two to recover.

## 5 MINUTE JOB

**Check the greenhouse heater** It's a job easily forgotten, but checking that your greenhouse insulation is still in place and the heater is working correctly can save you frustration in when spring comes along.

## IN THE FRUIT GARDEN

### Must-do jobs

**Remove mummified fruit** Now apple trees have lost their leaves, it's easy to spot any mummified fruit that have been affected by brown rot. Remove any you find and throw them away – council green waste collections will take them. Don't add them to your compost heap or it could spread the disease.

### Good to get done

**Plant new fruit trees and bushes** as long as the soil isn't frozen or wet. You'll find a good selection in garden centres, but for the widest choice of varieties buy from a specialist mail-order fruit nursery.

### Still time to ...

❋ **... tackle apple trees**, removing dead, diseased or crossing branches firs.

❋ **... prune vines** (see page 201).

**Plant bare-root hedging** For the best selection of varieties and the cheapest plants, it pays to buy bare-root hedging. Specialist nurseries offer the widest selection and most offer a mail-order service. But if you don't want to wait, most garden centres will also offer some bare-root plants at this time of year. If the ground is too frosty when you receive the plants, roughly plant them in a temporary spot, ready to move to their final position once conditions improve.

## ON THE VEG PATCH

### Must-do jobs

**Sow outdoors**

- Over-winter peas and broad beans

**Harvest**

- Carrots, parsnips, leeks
- Beetroot
- Brussels sprouts and sprouting broccoli
- Winter cabbage and cauliflower
- Winter salads

**Get digging** The warming glow that digging generates makes it the perfect job for a chilly winter day. It's a great way to improve soil by incorporating organic matter such as garden compost. Remember to stay off clay soils until the weather is dry.

### Good to get done

**Harvest winter brassicas** If you've got Brussels sprouts, pick them from the bottom of the plant upwards. Sprouting broccoli is another useful brassica and root crops, such as parsnips and carrots, and leeks can be lifted if the ground isn't too frosty.

**Check stored vegetables** Inspect stored strings of onions and garlic occasionally and remove any that are starting to rot or sprout. Also check your stored potatoes, especially if blight has been a problem – rotting tubers will give themselves away by a nasty smell. Remove these promptly.

## LAWNS

### Good to get done

**Give your lawn an instant lift** Recut any lawn edges that are looking particularly scruffy. It'll give your garden a lift – like having a haircut!

## PONDS

### Good to get done

**Stop your pond freezing** See the advice on page 205 for how to avoid your pond freezing over.

## HOW TO TAKE ROOT CUTTINGS

### WHAT YOU WILL NEED

❋ Sharp garden knife
❋ Multipurpose compost
❋ Sowing and cutting compost
❋ Growbag
❋ Dibber
❋ Pots/trays
❋ Horticultural grit

### What are they?
This is a very underrated technique that uses roots to create new plants. It's generally much easier than growing them from seed. It's mainly used on perennials, although some trees and shrubs such as Japanese quince and sumach are also suitable.

### When to do it?
From the end of October to the beginning of March.

**1** Dig up a plant or remove one from its pot. Look for roots that are firm and disease free. Cut them off close to the crown – don't take more than half the parent's roots.

### Some plants the technique is suitable for

Perennials such as:
❋ Oriental poppy
❋ Acanthus
❋ Japanese anemone
❋ Globe thistle
❋ Gypsophila
❋ Phlox
❋ Primulas

Woody plants such as:
❋ Tree of heaven (ailanthus)
❋ Japanese quince
❋ Oak-leafed hydrangea
❋ Sumach (rhus)

**2** Remove any fibrous lateral roots. Cut the root into 5-8cm lengths, making a horizontal cut across the top and a sloping cut at the bottom so it's easy to identify which end is which.

**3** Fill a pot with moistened compost. Make several holes using a dibber, and insert the cuttings horizontal cut facing up; the top of each cutting should be level with the surface.

**4** Cover with horticultural grit to provide good aeration for the buds that will develop in spring to early summer. Put the pot in a coldframe. Don't water until you see leafy growth.

**5** Pot up rooted cuttings individually and water them well. Once the new plant is established, it will be ready to plant out wherever you want it in the garden.

## Dealing with fine roots

With fine roots such as primula, it's best to use a seed tray instead of a pot. Cut the roots into longer sections (8–10cm long) than thicker roots and place them on the compost surface, rather than inserting them, and finally cover with horticultural grit.

# ▶ Index

index

# ▶ Credits